Pathways To The Past

Each volume stands alone as an Individual Book
Each volume stands together with others
to enhance the value of your collection

Build your Personal, Pastoral or Church Library
Pathways To The Past contains an ever-expanding list of
Christendom's most influential authors

Augustine of Hippo
Athanasius
E. M. Bounds
John Bunyan
Robert Lewis Darby
Brother Lawrence
Jessie Penn-Lewis
Bernard of Clairvaux
Andrew Murray
Watchman Nee
Arthur W. Pink
Thomas Watson
Hannah Whitall Smith
R. A. Torrey
A. W. Tozer
Jean-Pierre de Caussade
And many, many more.

THE
Barren Fig Tree;
OR,
The Doom and Downfall of the Fruitless Professor:
Showing, that the day of grace may be past with him long before his life is ended.
The signs also by which such miserable mortals may be known.

'Who being dead, yet speaketh.'—Hebrews 11:4

By *JOHN BUNYAN.*

LONDON,
Printed for J. Robinson, at the Golden Lion,
in St. Paul's Churchyard, *1688.*

The Barren Fig Tree;
John Bunyan

Published By Parables
December, 2019

All Rights Reserved. No part of this book may be reproduced or utilized in any form or by any means, electronic or mechanical, including photocopying, recording, or by any information storage and retrieval system, without permission in writing from the author.

    ISBN 978-1-951497-17-0
    Printed in the United States of America

Readers should be aware that Internet Web sites offered as citations and/or sources for further information may have been changed or disappeared between the time this was written and the time it is read.

THE
Barren Fig Tree;
OR,
The Doom and Downfall of the Fruitless Professor:
Showing, that the day of grace may be past with him long before his life is ended.
The signs also by which such miserable mortals may be known.

'Who being dead, yet speaketh.'—Hebrews 11:4

By *JOHN.BUNYAN.*

LONDON,
Printed for J. Robinson, at the Golden Lion,
in St. Paul's Churchyard, *1688.*

ADVERTISEMENT BY THE EDITOR

This solemn, searching, awful treatise, was published by Bunyan in 1682; but does not appear to have been reprinted until a very few months after his decease, which so unexpectedly took place in 1688. Although we have sought with all possible diligence, no copy of the first edition has been discovered; we have made use of a fine copy of the second edition, in possession of that thorough Bunyanite, my kind friend, R. B. Sherring, of Bristol. The third edition, 1692, is in the British Museum. Added to these posthumous publications appeared, for the first time, 'An Exhortation to Peace and Unity,' which will be found at the end of our second volume. In the advertisement to that treatise are stated, at some length, my reasons for concluding that it was not written by Bunyan, although inserted in all the editions of his collected works. That opinion is now more fully confirmed, by the discovery of Bunyan's own list of his works, published just before his death, in 1688, and in which that exhortation is not inserted. I was also much pleased to find that the same conclusion was arrived at by that highly intelligent Baptist minister, Mr. Robert Robinson.

His reasons are given at some length, concluding with, 'it is evident that Bunyan never wrote this piece.'[1] Why it was, after Bunyan's death, published with his 'Barren Fig-tree,' is one of those hidden mysteries of darkness and of wickedness that I cannot discover. The beautiful parable from which Bunyan selected his text, represents an enclosed ground, in which, among others, a fig-tree had been planted. It was not an enclosure similar to some of the vineyards of France or Germany, exclusively devoted to the growth of the vine, but a garden in which fruits were cultivated, such as grapes, figs, or pomegranates. It was in such a vineyard, thus retired from the world, that Nathaniel poured out his heart in prayer, when our Lord in spirit witnessed, unseen, these devotional exercises, and soon afterwards rewarded him with open approbation (John 1:48). In these secluded pleasant spots the Easterns spend much of their time, under their own vines or fig-trees, sheltered from the world and from the oppressive heat of the sun—a fit emblem of a church of Christ. In this vineyard stood a fig-tree—by nature remarkable for fruitfulness—but it is barren. No inquiry is made as to how it came there, but the order is given, 'Cut it down.' The dresser of the garden intercedes, and means are tried to make it fruitful, but in vain. At last it is cut down as a cumber-ground and burnt. This vineyard or garden represents a gospel church; the fig-tree a member— a barren, fruitless professor. 'It matters not how he got there,' if he bears no fruit he must be cut down and away to the fire.

To illustrate so awful a subject this treatise was written, and it is intensely solemn. God, whose omniscience penetrates through every disguise, himself examines every tree in the garden, yea, every bough. Wooden and earthy professor, your detection is sure; appearances that deceive the world and the church cannot deceive God. 'He will be with thee in thy bed fruits—thy midnight fruits—thy closet fruits— thy family fruits—they conversation fruits.' Professor, solemnly examine yourself; 'in proportion to your fruitfulness will be your blessedness.' 'Naked and open are all things to his eye.' Can it be imagined that those 'that paint themselves did ever repent of their pride?' 'How seemingly self-denying are some of these creeping things.' 'Is there no place will serve to fit those for hell but the church, the vineyard of God?' 'It is not the place where the worker of iniquity can hide himself or his sins from God.' May such be detected before they go hence to the fire. While there is a disposition to seek grace all are invited to come; but when salvation by Christ is abandoned, there is no other refuge, although sought with tears. Reader, may the deeply impressive language of Bunyan sink profoundly into our hearts. We need no splendid angel nor hideous demon to reveal to us the realities of the world to come. 'If we hear not Moses and the prophets,' as set forth by Bunyan in this treatise, 'neither should we be persuaded though one rose from the dead' to declare these solemn truths (Luke 16:31).

GEO. OFFOR.

John Bunyan

TO THE READER.

COURTEOUS READER,

I have written to thee now about the Barren Fig-tree, or how it will fare with the fruitless professor that standeth in the vineyard of God. Of what complexion thou art I cannot certainly divine; but the parable tells thee that the cumber- ground must be cut down. A cumber-ground professor is not only a provocation to God, a stumbling-block to the world, and a blemish to religion, but a snare to his own soul also. 'Though his excellency mount up to the heavens, and his head reach unto the clouds, yet he shall perish for ever, like his own dung; they which have seen him shall say, Where is he?' (Job 20:6,7).

Now 'they count it pleasure to riot in the daytime.' But what will they do when the axe is fetched out? (2 Peter 2:13,14).

The tree whose fruit withereth is reckoned a tree without fruit, a tree twice dead, one that must be 'plucked up by the roots' (Jude 12).

O thou cumber-ground, God expects fruit, God will come seeking fruit shortly.

My exhortation, therefore, is to professors that they look to it, that they take heed.

The barren fig-tree in the vineyard, and the bramble in the wood, are both prepared for the fire.

Profession is not a covert to hide from the eye of God; nor will it palliate the revengeful threatening of his justice; he will command to cut it down shortly.

The church, and a profession, are the best of places for the upright, but the worst in the world for the cumber-ground. He must be cast, as profane, out of the mount of God: cast, I say, over the wall of the vineyard, there to wither; thence to be gathered and burned. 'It had ben better for them not to have known the way of righteousness' (2 Peter 2:21). And yet if they had not, they had been damned; but it is better to go to hell without, than in, or from under a profession. These 'shall receive greater damnation' (Luke 20:47).

If thou be a professor, read and tremble: if thou be profane, do so likewise. For if the righteous scarcely be saved, where shall the ungodly and sinners appear? Cumber- ground, take heed of the axe! Barren fig-tree, beware of the fire!

But I will keep thee no longer out of the book. Christ Jesus, the dresser of the vineyard, take care of thee, dig about thee, and dung thee, that thou mayest bear fruit; that when the Lord of the vineyard cometh with his axe to seek for fruit, or pronounce the sentence of damnation on the barren fig-tree, thou mayest escape that judgment. The cumber- ground must to the wood-pile, and thence to the fire. Farewell.

Grace be with all them that love our Lord Jesus in sincerity. Amen.

JOHN BUNYAN

THE BARREN FIG-TREE, OR THE DOOM AND DOWNFALL OF THE FRUITLESS PROFESSOR.

'A CERTAIN MAN HAD A FIG-TREE PLANTED IN HIS VINEYARD; AND HE CAME AND SOUGHT FRUIT THEREON, AND FOUND NONE. THEN SAID HE UNTO THE DRESSER OF HIS VINEYARD, BEHOLD, THESE THREE YEARS I COME SEEKING FRUIT ON THE FIG-TREE, AND FIND NONE: CUT IT DOWN; WHY CUMBERETH IT THE GROUND? AND HE ANSWERING SAID UNTO HIM, LORD, LET IT ALONE THIS YEAR ALSO, TILL I SHALL DIG ABOUT IT, AND DUNG IT: AND IF IT BEAR FRUIT, WELL: AND IF NOT, THEN AFTER THAT THOU SHALT CUT IT DOWN.'—LUKE 13:6-9.

At the beginning of this chapter we read how some of the Jews came to Jesus Christ, to tell him of the cruelty of Pontius Pilate, in mingling the blood of the Galileans with their sacrifices. A heathenish and prodigious act; for therein he showed, not only his malice against the Jewish nation, but also against their worship, and consequently their God. An action, I say, not only heathenish, but prodigious also; for the Lord Jesus, paraphrasing upon this fact of his, teacheth the Jews, that without repentance 'they should all likewise perish.' 'Likewise,' that is by the hand and rage of the Roman empire. Neither should they be more able to avoid the stroke, than were those eighteen upon whom the tower of Siloam fell, and slew them (Luke 13:1-5). The fulfilling of which prophecy, for their hardness of heart, and impenitency, was in the days of Titus, son of Vespasian, about forty years after the death of Christ. Then, I say, were these Jews, and their city, both environed round on every side, wherein both they and it, to amazement, were miserably overthrown. God gave them sword and famine, pestilence and blood, for their outrage against the Son of his love. So wrath 'came upon them to the uttermost' (1 Thess 2:16).[2]

Now, to prevent their old and foolish salvo, which they always had in readiness against such prophecies and denunciations of judgment, the Lord Jesus presents them with this parable, in which he emphatically shows them that their cry of being the temple of the Lord, and of their being the children of Abraham, &c., and their being the church of God, would not stand them in any stead. As who should say, It may be you think to help yourselves against this my prophecy of your utter and unavoidable overthrow, by the interest which you have in your outward privileges. But all these will fail you; for what think you? 'A certain man had a fig-tree planted in his vineyard, and he came and sought fruit thereon, and found none.' This is your case! The Jewish land is God's vineyard; I know it; and I know also, that you are the fig-trees. But behold, there wanteth the main thing, fruit; for the sake, and in expectation of which, he set this vineyard with trees. Now, seeing the fruit is not found amongst you, the fruit, I say, for the sake of which he did at first plant this vineyard, what remains but that in justice he command to cut you down as those that cumber the ground, that he may plant himself another vineyard? 'Then said he unto the dresser of his vineyard, Behold, these three years I come seeking fruit on this fig-tree, and find none; cut it down, why cumbereth it the ground?' This therefore must be your end, although you are planted in the garden of God; for the barrenness and unfruitfulness of your hearts and lives you must be cut off, yea, rooted up, and cast out of the vineyard.

In parables there are two things to be taken notice of, and to be inquired into of them that read. First, The metaphors made use of. Second, The doctrine or mysteries couched under such metaphors.

The metaphors in this parable are, 1. A certain man; 2. A vineyard; 3. A fig-tree, barren or fruitless; 4. A dresser; 5. Three years; 6. Digging and dunging, &c.

The doctrine, or mystery, couched under these words is to show us what is like to become of a fruitless or formal professor. For, 1. By the man in the parable is meant God the Father (Luke 15:11). 2. By the vineyard, his church (Isa 5:7). 3. By the fig-tree, a professor. 4. By the dresser, the Lord Jesus. 5. By the fig-tree's barrenness, the professor's fruitlessness. 6. By the three years, the patience of God that for a time he extendeth to barren professors. 7. This calling to the dresser of the vineyard to cut it down, is to show the outcries of justice against fruitless professors. 8. The dresser's interceding is to show how the Lord Jesus steps in, and takes hold of the head of his Father's axe, to stop, or at least to defer, the present execution of a barren fig-tree. 9. The dresser's desire to try to make the fig-tree fruitful, is to show you how unwilling he is that even a barren fig-tree should yet be barren, and perish. 10. His digging about it, and dunging of it, is to show his willingness to apply gospel helps to this barren professor, if haply he may be fruitful. 11. The supposition that the fig-tree may yet continue fruitless, is to show, that when Christ Jesus hath done all, there are some professors will abide barren and fruitless. 12. The determination upon this supposition, at last to cut it down, is a certain prediction of such professor's unavoidable and eternal damnation.

But to take this parable into pieces, and to discourse more particularly, though with all brevity, upon all the parts thereof.

'A certain MAN had a fig-tree planted in his vineyard.'

The MAN, I told you, is to present us with God the Father; by which similitude he is often set out in the New Testament.

Observe then, that it is no new thing, if you find in God's church barren fig-trees, fruitless professors; even as here you see is a tree, a fruitless tree, a fruitless fig-tree in the vineyard.[3] Fruit is not so easily brought forth as a profession is got into; it is easy for a man to clothe himself with a fair show in the flesh, to word it, and say, Be thou warmed and filled with the best. It is no hard thing to do these with other things; but to be fruitful, to bring forth fruit to God, this doth not every tree, no not every fig-tree that stands in the vineyard of God. Those words also, 'Every branch in me that beareth not fruit, he taketh away,' assert the same thing (John 15:2). There are branches in Christ, in Christ's body mystical, which is his church, his vineyard, that bear not fruit, wherefore the hand of God is to take them away: I looked for grapes, and it brought forth wild grapes, that is, no fruit at all that was acceptable with God (Isa 5:4). Again, 'Israel is an empty vine, he bringeth forth fruit unto himself,' none to God; he is without fruit to God (Hosea 10:1). All these, with many more, show us the truth of the observation, and that God's church may be cumbered with fruitless fig-trees, with barren professors.

Had a FIG-TREE.

Although there be in God's church that be barren and fruitless; yet, as I said, to see to, they are like the rest of the trees, even a fig-tree. It was not an oak, nor a willow, nor a thorn, nor a bramble; but a FIG-TREE. 'they come unto thee as the people cometh' (Eze 33:31). 'They delight to know my ways, as a nation that did righteousness, and forsook not the ordinance of their God. They ask of me the ordinances of justice, they take delight in approaching to God,' and yet but barren, fruitless, and unprofitable professors (Isa 58:2-4). Judas also was one of the twelve, a disciple, an apostle, a preacher, an officer, yea, and such a one as none of the eleven mistrusted, but preferred before themselves, each one crying out, 'Is it I? Is it I?' (Mark 14:19). None of them, as we read of (John 6:70), mistrusting Judas; yet he in Christ's eye was the barren fig-tree, a devil, a fruitless professor. The foolish virgins also went forth of the world with the other, had lamps, and light, and were awakened with the other; yea, had boldness to go forth, when the midnight cry was made, with the other; and thought that they could have looked Christ in the face, when he sat upon the throne of judgment, with the other; and yet but foolish, but barren fig-trees, but fruitless professors. 'Many,' saith Christ, 'will say unto me in that day,' this and that, and will also talk of many wonderful works; yet, behold, he finds nothing in them but the fruits of unrighteousness (Matt 7:22,23). They were altogether barren and fruitless professors.

Had a fig-tree PLANTED.

This word PLANTED doth also reach far; it supposeth one taken out of its natural soil, or removed from the place it grew in once; one that seemed to be called, awakened; and not only so, but by strong hand carried from the world to the church; from nature to grace; from sin to godliness. 'Thou hast brought a vine out of Egypt; thou hast cast out the heathen, and planted it' (Psa 80:8). Of some of the branches of this vine were there unfruitful professors.

It must be concluded, therefore, that this professor, that remaineth notwithstanding fruitless, is, as to the view and judgment of the church, rightly brought in thither, to wit, by confession of faith, of sin, and a show of repentance and regeneration; thus false brethren creep in unawares![4] All these things this word planted intimateth; yea, further, that the church is satisfied with them, consents they should abide in the garden, and counteth them sound as the rest. But before God, in the sight of God, they are graceless professors, barren and fruitless fig-trees.

Therefore it is one thing to be in the church, or in a profession; and another to be of the church, and to belong to that kingdom that is prepared for the saint, that is so indeed. Otherwise, 'Being planted, shall it prosper? shall it not utterly wither, when the east-wind toucheth it? It shall wither in the furrows where it grew' (Eze 17:10).

Had a fig-tree planted in HIS vineyard.

In HIS vineyard. Hypocrites, with rotten hearts, are not afraid to come before God in Sion. These words therefore suggest unto us a prodigious kind of boldness and hardened fearlessness. For what presumption higher, and what attempt more desperate, than for a man that wanteth grace, and the true knowledge of God, to crowd himself, in that condition, into the house or church of God; or to make profession of, and desire that the name of God should be called upon him?

For the man that maketh a profession of the religion of Jesus Christ, that man hath, as it were, put the name of God upon himself, and is called and reckoned now, how fruitless soever before God or men, the man that hath to do with God, the man that God owneth, and will stand for. This man, I say, by his profession, suggesteth this to all that know him to be such a professor. Men merely natural, I mean men that have not got the devilish art of hypocrisy, are afraid to think of doing thus. 'And of the rest durst no man join himself to them; but the people magnified them' (Acts 5:13). And, indeed, it displeaseth God. 'Ye have brought,' saith he, 'men uncircumcised into my sanctuary' (Eze 44:7). And again, 'When ye come to appear before me, who hath required this at your hand, to tread my courts?' saith God (Isa 1:12). They have therefore learned this boldness of none in the visible world, they only took it of the devil, for he, and he only, with these his disciples, attempt to present themselves in the church before God. 'The tares are the children of the wicked one.' The tares, that is, the hypocrites, that are Satan's brood, the generation of vipers, that cannot escape the damnation of hell.

HAD a fig-tree planted in his vineyard.

He doth not say, He planted a fig-tree, but there was a fig-tree there; he HAD, or found a fig-tree planted in his vineyard.

The great God will now acknowledge the barren fig-tree, or barren professor, to be his workmanship, or a tree of his bringing in, only the text saith, he had one there. This is much like that in Matthew 15:13—'Every plant which my heavenly Father hath not planted, shall be rooted up.' Here again are plants in his vineyard which God will not acknowledge to be of his planting; and he seems to suggest that in his vineyard are many such. Every plant, or all those plants or professors, that are got into the assembly of the saints, or into the profession of their religion, without God and his grace, 'shall be rooted up.'

'And when the King came in to see the guests, he saw there a man which had not on the wedding-garment. And he saith unto him, Friend, how camest thou in hither, not having a wedding-garment?' (Matt 22:11,12). Here is one so cunning and crafty that he beguiled all the guests; he got and kept in the church even until the King himself came in to see the guests; but his subtilty got him nothing; it did not blind the eyes of the King; it did not pervert the judgment of the righteous. 'Friend, how camest thou in hither?' did overtake him at last; even a public rejection; the King discovered him in the face of all present. 'How camest thou in hither?' My Father did not bring thee hither; I did not bring thee hither; my Spirit did not bring thee hither; thou art not of the heavenly Father's planting. 'How camest thou in hither?' He that 'entereth not by the door, but climbeth up some other way, the same is a thief and a robber' (John 10:1). This text also is full and plain to our purpose; for this man came not in by the door, yet got into the church; he got in by climbing; he broke in at the windows; he got something of the light and glory of the gospel of our Lord Jesus Christ in his head; and so, hardy wretch that he was, he presumed to crowd himself among the children. But how is this resented? What saith the King of him? Why, this is his sign, 'the same is a thief and a robber.' See ye here also, if all they be owned as the planting of God that get into his church or profession of his name.

'Had a fig-tree.' Had one without a wedding-garment, had a thief in his garden, at his wedding, in his house. These climbed up some other way. There are many ways to get into the church of God, and profession of his name, besides, and without an entering by the door.

1. There is the way of lying and dissembling, and at this gap the Gibeonites got in (Josh 9 &c).

2. There is sometimes falseness among some pastors, either for the sake of carnal relations, or the like; at this hole Tobiah, the enemy of God, got in (Neh 13:4-9).

3. There is sometimes negligence, and too much uncircumspectness in the whole church; thus the uncircumcised got in (Eze 44:7,8).

4. Sometimes, again, let the church be never so circumspect, yet these have so much help from the devil that they beguile them all, and so get in. These are of the sort of thieves that Paul complains of, 'False brethren, that are brought in unawares' (Gal 2:4). Jude also cries out of these, 'Certain men crept in unawares' (Jude 4). Crept in! What, were they so lowly? A voluntary humility, a neglecting of the body, not in any humour (Col 2:23).[5] O! how seemingly self-denying are some of these 'creeping things,' that yet are to be held, (as we shall know them) an abomination to Israel (Lev 11:43,44).

But in a great house there are not only vessels of gold and of silver, but also of wood and of earth; and some to honour, and some to dishonour (2 Tim 2:20). By these words the apostle seems to take it for granted, that as there hath been, so there still will be these kind of fig-trees, these barren professors in the house, when all men have done what they can; even as in a great house there are always vessels to dishonour, as well as those to honour and glory; vessels of wood and of earth, as well as of silver and gold. So, then, there must be wooden professors in the garden of God, there must be earthy, earthen professors in his vineyard; but that methinks is the biting word, 'and some to dishonour' (Rom 9:21,22). That to the Romans is dreadful, but this seems to go beyond it; that speaks but of the reprobate in general, but this of such and such in particular; that speaks of their hardening but in the common way, but this that they must be suffered to creep into the church, there to fit themselves for their place, their own place, the place prepared for them of this sort only (Acts 1:25). As the Lord Jesus said once of the Pharisees, These 'shall receive greater damnation' (Luke 20:47).

Barren fig-tree, fruitless professor, hast thou heard all these things? Hast thou considered that this fig-tree is not acknowledged of God to be his, but is denied to be of his planting, and of his bringing unto his wedding? Dost not thou see that thou art called a thief and a robber, that hast either climbed up to, or crept in at another place than the door? Dost thou not hear that there will be in God's house wooden and earthly professors, and that no place will serve to fit those for hell but the house, the church, the vineyard of God? Barren fig-tree, fruitless Christian, do not thine ears tingle?

And HE came and sought fruit thereon.

When a man hath got a profession, and is crowded into the church and house of God, the question is not now, Hath he life, hath he right principles? but, Hath he fruit? HE came seeking fruit thereon. It mattereth not who brought thee in hither, whether God or the devil, or thine own vain-glorious heart; but hast thou fruit? Dost thou bring forth fruit unto God? And, 'Let every one that nameth the name of' the Lord Jesus 'Christ depart from iniquity' (2 Tim 2:19). He doth not say, And let every one that hath grace, or let those that have the Spirit of God; but, 'Let every one that nameth the name of' the Lord Jesus 'Christ depart form iniquity.'

What do men meddle with religion for? Why do they call themselves by the name of the Lord Jesus, if they have not the grace of God, if they have not the Spirit of Christ? God, therefore, expecteth fruit. What do they do in the vineyard? Let them work, or get them out; the vineyard must have labourers in it. 'Son, go WORK to-day in my vineyard' (Matt 21:28). Wherefore, want of grace and want of Spirit will not keep God from seeking fruit. 'And he came and sought fruit thereon' (Luke 13:6, 8:8). He requireth that which he seemeth to have. Every man in the vineyard and house of God promiseth himself, professeth to others, and would have all men take it for granted, that a heavenly principle is in him, why then should not God seek fruit?

As for them, therefore, that will retain the name of Christians, fearing God, and yet make no conscience of bringing forth fruit to him, he saith to such, Away! 'As for you, - Go ye, serve ye every one his idols, and hereafter also, if ye will not hearken unto me,' &c. (Eze 20:39). Barren fig-tree, dost thou hear? God expecteth fruit, God calls for fruit, yea, God will shortly come seeking fruit on this barren fig-tree. Barren fig-tree, either bear fruit, or go out of the vineyard; and yet then thy case will be unspeakably damnable. Yea, let me add, if thou shalt neither bear fruit nor depart, God will take his name out of thy mouth (Jer 44:26). He will have fruit. And I say further, if thou wilt do neither, yet God in justice and righteousness will still come for fruit. And it will be in vain for thee to count this austerity. He will reap where he hath not sowed, and gather where he hath not strewed (Matt 25:24-26). Barren fig-tree, dost thou hear?

Quest. What if a man have no grace?

Answ. Yes, seeing he hath a profession.

And he came and sought fruit THEREON.

A church, then, and a profession, are not places where the workers of iniquity may hide themselves and sins from God. Some of old thought that because they could cry, 'The temple of the Lord, the temple of the Lord!' that therefore they were delivered, or had a dispensation to do the abominations which they committed, as some in our days; for who, say they, have a right to the creatures, if not Christians, if not professors, if not church members? And, from this conclusion, let go the reins of their inordinate affections after pride, ambition, gluttony; pampering themselves without fear (Jude 12), daubing themselves with the lust-provoking fashions of the times; to walk with stretched out necks, naked breasts, frizzled fore-tops, wanton gestures, in gorgeous apparel, mixed with gold and pearl, and costly array.[6] I will not here make inspection into their lives, their carriages at home, in their corners and secret holes; but certainly, persons thus spirited, thus principled, and thus inclined, have but empty boughs, boughs that want the fruit that God expects, and that God will come down to seek.

Barren fig-tree, thou art not licensed by thy profession, nor by the Lord of the vineyard, to bear these clusters of Gomorrah; neither shall the vineyard, nor thy being crowded among the trees there, shelter thee from the sight of the eye of God. Many make religion their cloak, and Christ their stalking-horse, and by that means cover themselves and hide their own wickedness from men; but God seeth their hearts, hath his print upon the heels of their feet, and pondereth all their goings; and at last, when their iniquity is found to be hateful, he will either smite them with hardness of heart, and so leave them, or awaken them to bring forth fruit. Fruit he looks for, seeks, and expects, barren fig-tree!

But what! come into the presence of God to sin! What! come into the presence of God to hide thy sin! Alas, man! the church is God's garden, and Christ Jesus is the great Apostle and High-priest of our profession. What! come into the house that is called by my name! into the place where mine honour dwelleth! (Psa 26:8). Where mine eyes and heart are continually! (1 Kings 9:3). What! come there to sin, to hide thy sin, to cloak thy sin! His plants are an orchard with pleasant fruits (Cant 4:13). And every time he goeth into his garden, it is to see the fruits of the valley, and to 'see if the vine flourished, and the pomegranates budded.'

Yea, saith he, he came seeking fruit on this fig-tree. The church is the place of God's delight, where he ever desires to be: there he is night and day. He is there to seek for fruit, to seek for fruit of all and every tree in the garden. Wherefore, assure thyself, O fruitless one, that thy ways must needs be open before the eyes of the Lord. One black sheep is soon espied, although in company with many; that is taken with the first cast of the eye; its different colour still betrays it. I say, therefore, a church and a profession are not places where the workers of iniquity may hide themselves from God that seeks for fruit. 'My vineyard,' saith God, 'which is mine, is before me' (Cant 8:12).

And he came and sought fruit thereon, AND FOUND NONE.

Barren fig-tree, hearken; the continual non-bearing of fruit is a dreadful sign that thou art to come to a dreadful end, as the winding up of this parable concludeth.

'AND FOUND NONE.' None at all, or none to God's liking; for when he saith, 'He came seeking fruit thereon,' he means 'fruit meet for God,' pleasant fruit, fruit good and sweet (Heb 6). Alas! it is not any fruit will serve; bad fruit is counted none. 'Every tree which bringeth not forth good fruit is hewn down, and cast into the fire' (Matt 3:10).

First. There is a fruit among professors that withers, and so never comes to be ripe; a fruit that is smitten in the growth, and comes not to maturity; and this is reckoned no fruit. This fruit those professors bear that have many fair beginnings, or blossoms; that make many fair offers of repentance and amendment; that begin to pray, to resolve, and to break off their sins by righteousness, but stop at those beginnings, and bring not fruit forth to perfection. This man's fruit is withered, wrinkled, smitten fruit, and is in effect no fruit at all.

Second. There is a hasty fruit, such as is the 'corn upon the house-top' (Psa 129:6); or that which springs up on the dung-hill, that runs up suddenly, violently, with great stalks and big show, and yet at last proves empty of kernel. This fruit is to be found in those professors that on a sudden are so awakened, so convinced, and so affected with their condition that they shake the whole family, the endship,[7] the whole town. For a while they cry hastily, vehemently, dolefully, mournfully, and yet all is but a pang, an agony, a fit, they bring not forth fruit with patience. These are called those hasty fruits that 'shall be a fading flower' (Isa 28:4).

Third. There is a fruit that is vile and ill-tasted, how long soever it be in growing; the root is dried, and cannot convey a sufficiency of sap to the branches, to ripen the fruit (Jer 24). These are the fruits of such professors whose hearts are estranged from communion with the Holy Ghost, whose fruit groweth from themselves, from their parts, gifts, strength of wit, natural or moral principles. These, notwithstanding they bring forth fruit, are called empty vines, such as bring not forth fruit to God. 'Their root is dried up, they shall bear no fruit; yea, though they bring forth, yet will I slay even the beloved fruit of their womb' (Hosea 9:16).

Fourth. There is a fruit that is wild. 'I looked for grapes and it brought forth wild grapes' (Isa 5:4). I observe, that as there are trees and herbs that are wholly right and noble, fit indeed for the vineyard; so there are also their semblance, but wild; not right, but ignoble. There is the grape, and the wild grape; the vine, and the wild vine; the rose, and canker rose; flowers and wild flowers; the apple, and the wild apple which we call the crab. Now, fruit from these wild things, however they may please the children to play with, yet the prudent and grave count them of little or no value. There are also in the world a generation of professors that, notwithstanding their profession, are wild by nature; yea, such as were never cut out, or off, from the wild olive-tree, nor never yet planted into the good olive-tree. Now, these can bring nothing forth but wild olive berries, they cannot bring forth fruit unto God. Such are all those that have lightly taken up a profession, and crept into the vineyard without a new birth, and the blessing of regeneration.

Fifth. There is also untimely fruit: 'Even as a fig-tree casteth her untimely figs' (Rev 6, 13). Fruit out of season, and so no fruit to God's liking. There are two sorts of professors subject to bring forth untimely fruit: 1. They that bring forth fruit too soon; 2. They that bring forth fruit too late.

1. They that bring forth too soon. They are such as at present receive the Word with joy; and anon, before they have root downwards, they thrust forth upwards; but having not root, when the sun ariseth, they are smitten, and miserably die without fruit. These professors are those light and inconsiderate ones that think nothing but peace will attend the gospel; and so anon rejoice at the tidings, without foreseeing the evil. Wherefore, when the evil comes, being unarmed, and so not able to stand any longer, they die, and are withered, and bring forth no fruit. 'He that received the seed into stony places, the same is he that heareth the Word, and anon with joy receiveth it; yet hath he not root in himself, but dureth for a while; for when tribulation or persecution ariseth because of the Word, by and by he is offended' (Matt 13:20,21). There is, in Isaiah 28:4, mention made of some 'whose glorious beauty shall be a fading flower,' because it is 'fruit before the summer.' Both these are untimely fruit.

2. They also bring forth untimely fruit that stay till the season is over. God will have his fruit in his season; I say, he will receive them of such men as shall render them to him in their seasons (Matt 21:41). The missing of the season is dangerous; staying till the door is shut is dangerous (Matt 25:10,11). Many there be that come not till the flood of God's anger is raised, and too deep for them to wade through; 'Surely in the floods of great waters they shall not come nigh unto him' (Psa 32:6). Esau AFTERWARDS is fearful: 'For ye know how that afterward, when he would have inherited the blessing, he was rejected; for he found no place of repentance, though he sought it carefully with tears' (Heb 12:17).

So the children of Israel, they brought to God the fruits of obedience too late; their 'Lo, we be here' came too late (Num 14:40-42); their

'We will go up' came too late (Num 14:40-44). The Lord had sworn before, 'that they should not possess the land' (Matt 25:10, 27:5). All these are such as bring forth untimely fruit (Heb 12:17; Luke 13:25-27). It is the hard hap of the reprobate to do all things too late; to be sensible of his want of grace too late; to be sorry for sin too late; to seek repentance too late; to ask for mercy, and to desire to go to glory too late.

Thus you see, 1. That fruit smitten in the growth, that withereth, and that comes not to maturity, is no fruit. 2. That hasty fruit, such as 'the grass upon the house-top,' withereth also before it groweth up, and is no fruit (Psa 129:6). 3. That the fruit that is vile, and ill-tasted, is no fruit. That wild fruit, wild grapes, are no fruit (Rev 6). That untimely fruit, such as comes too soon, or that comes too late, such as come not in their season, are no fruit.

And he came and sought FRUIT thereon, and found none.

Nothing will do but fruit; he looked for grapes. 'When the time of the fruit drew near, he sent his servants to the husbandmen, that they might receive the fruits of it' (Matt 21:34).

Quest. But what fruit doth God expect?

Answ. Good fruit. 'Every tree that bringeth not forth good fruit, is hewn down' (Matt 7:19). Now, before the fruit can be good, the tree must be good; for good fruit makes not a good tree, but a 'good tree bringeth forth good fruit. Do men gather grapes of thorns, or figs of thistles?' A man must be good, else he can bring forth no good fruit; he must have righteousness imputed, that he may stand good in God;'s sight from the curse of his law; he must have a principle of righteousness in his soul, else how should he bring forth good fruits? and hence it is, that a Christian's fruits are called 'the fruits of the Spirit, the fruits of righteousness, which are by Jesus Christ' (Gal 5:22,23; Phil 1:11). The fruits of the Spirit, therefore the Spirit must be there; the fruits of righteousness, therefore righteousness must first be there. But to particularize in a few things briefly:—

First. God expecteth fruit that will answer, and be worthy of the repentance which thou feignest thyself to have. Every one in a profession, and that hath crowded into the vineyard, pretendeth to repentance; now of every such soul, God expecteth that the fruits of repentance be found to attend them. 'Bring forth, therefore, fruits meet for repentance,' or answerable to thy profession of the doctrine of repentance (Matt 3:8). Barren fig-tree, seeing thou art a professor, and art got into the vineyard, thou standest before the Lord of the vineyard as one of the trees of the garden; wherefore he looketh for fruit from thee, as from the rest of the trees in the vineyard; fruits, I say, and such as may declare thee in heart and life one that hath made sound profession of repentance. By thy profession thou hast said, I am sensible of the evil of sin. Now then, live such a life as declares that thou art sensible of the evil of sin. By thy profession thou hast said, I am sorry for my sin. Why, then, live such a life as may declare this sorrow. By thy profession thou hast said, I am ashamed of my sin; yea, but live such a life, that men by that may see thy shame for sin (Psa 38:18; Jer 31:19). By thy profession thou sayest, I have turned from, left off, and am become an enemy to every appearance of evil (1 Thess 5:22). Ah! but doth thy life and conversation declare thee to be such an one? Take heed, barren fig-tree, lest thy life should give thy profession the lie. I say again, take heed, for God himself will come for fruit. 'And he sought fruit thereon.'

You have some professors that are only saints before men when they are abroad, but are devils and vipers at home; saints by profession, but devils by practice; saints in word, but sinners in heart and life. These men may have the profession, but they want the fruits that become repentance.[8]

Barren fig-tree, can it be imagined that those that paint themselves did ever repent of their pride? or that those that pursue this world did ever repent of their covetousness? or that those that walk with wanton eyes did ever repent of their fleshly lusts? Where, barren fig-tree, is the fruit of these people's repentance? Nay, do they not rather declare to the world that they have repented of their profession? Their fruits look as if they had. Their pride saith they have repented of their humility. Their covetousness declareth that they are weary of depending upon God; and doth not thy wanton actions declare that thou abhorrest chastity? Where is thy fruit, barren fig-tree? Repentance is not only a sorrow, and a shame for, but a turning from sin to God; it is called 'repentance from dead works' (Heb 6:1). Hast thou that 'godly sorrow' that 'worketh repentance to salvation, not to be repented of?' (2 Cor 7:10,11). How dost thou show thy carefulness, and clearing of thyself; thy indignation against sin; they fear of offending; thy vehement desire to walk with God; thy zeal for his name and glory in the world? And what revenge hast thou in thy heart against every thought of disobedience?

But where is the fruit of this repentance? Where is thy watching, thy fasting, thy praying against the remainders of corruption? Where is thy self-abhorrence, thy blushing before God, for the sin that is yet behind? Where is thy tenderness of the name of God and his ways? Where is thy self-denial and contentment? How dost thou show before men the truth of thy turning to God? Hast thou 'renounced the hidden things of dishonesty, not walking in craftiness?' Canst thou commend thyself 'to every man's conscience in the sight of God?' (2 Cor 4:2).

Second. God expecteth fruits that shall answer that faith which thou makest profession of. The professor that is got into the vineyard of God doth feign that he hath the faith, the faith most holy, the faith of God's elect. Ah! but where are thy fruits, barren fig-tree? The faith of the Romans was 'spoken of throughout the whole world' (Rom 1:8). And the Thessalonians' faith grew exceedingly (2 Thess 1:3).

Thou professest to believe thou hast a share in another world: hast thou let got THIS, barren fig-tree? Thou professest thou believest in Christ: is he thy joy, and the life of thy soul? Yea, what conformity unto him, to his sorrows and sufferings? What resemblance hath his crying, and groaning, and bleeding, and dying, wrought in thee? Dost thou 'bear about in thy body the dying of the Lord Jesus?' and is also the life of Jesus 'made manifest in thy mortal body?' (2 Cor 4:10,11). Barren fig-tree, 'show me thy faith by thy works.' 'Show out of a good conversation thy works with meekness of wisdom' (James 2:18, 3:13). What fruit, barren fig-tree, what degree of heart holiness? for faith purifies the heart (Acts 15:9). What love to the Lord Jesus? for 'faith worketh by love' (Gal 5:6).

Third. God expecteth fruits according to the seasons of grace thou art under, according to the rain that cometh upon thee. Perhaps thou art planted in a good soil, by great waters, that thou mightest bring forth branches, and bear fruit; that thou mightest be a goodly vine or fig-tree. Shall he not therefore seek for fruit, for fruit answerable to the means? Barren fig-tree, God expects it, and will find it too, if ever he bless thee. 'For the earth which drinketh in the rain that cometh oft upon it, and bringeth forth herbs meet for them by whom it is dressed, receiveth blessing from God: but that which beareth thorns and briars is rejected, and is nigh unto cursing, whose end is to be burned' (Heb 6:7,8).

Barren soul, how many showers of grace, how many dews from heaven, how many times have the silver streams of the city of God run gliding by thy roots, to cause thee to bring forth fruit! These showers and streams, and the drops that hang upon thy boughs, will all be accounted for; and will they not testify against thee that thou oughtest, of right, to be burned? Hear and tremble, O thou barren professor! Fruits that become thy profession of the gospel, the God of heaven expecteth. The gospel hath in it the forgiveness of sins, the kingdom of heaven, and eternal life; but what fruit hath thy profession of a belief of these things put forth in thy heart and life? Hast thou given thyself to the Lord? and is all that thou hast to be ventured for his name in this world? Dost thou walk like one that is bought with a price, even with the price of precious blood?

Fourth. The fruit that God expecteth is such as is meet for himself; fruit that may glorify God. God's trees are trees of righteousness, the planting of the Lord, that he may be glorified; fruit that tasteth of heaven, abundance of such fruit. For 'herein,' saith Christ, 'is my Father glorified, that ye bear much fruit' (John 15:8). Fruits of all kinds, new and old; the fruits of the Spirit are in all goodness, and righteousness, and truth. Fruits before the world, fruits before the saints, fruits before God, fruits before angels.

O my brethren, 'what manner of persons ought we to be,' who have subscribed to the Lord, and have called ourselves by the name of Israel? 'One shall say I am the Lord's; and another shall call himself by the name of Jacob; and another shall subscribe with his hand unto the Lord, and surname himself by the name of Israel' (Isa 44:5). Barren fig-tree, hast thou subscribed, hast thou called thyself by the name of Jacob, and surnamed thyself by the name of Israel? All this thou pretendest to, who art got into the vineyard, who art placed among the trees of the garden of God. God doth therefore look for such fruit as is worthy of his name, as is meet for him; as the apostle saith, 'we should walk worthy of God'; that is, so as we may show in every place that the presence of God is with us, his fear in us, and his majesty and authority upon our actions. Fruits meet for him, such a dependence upon him, such trust in his word, such satisfaction in his presence, such a trusting of him with all my concerns, and such delight in the enjoyment of him, that may demonstrate that his fear is in my heart, that my soul is wrapped up in his things, and that my body, and soul, and estate, and all, are in truth, through his grace, at his dispose, fruit meet for him. Hearty thanks, and blessing God for Jesus Christ, for his good word, for his free grace, for the discovery of himself in Christ to the soul, secret longing after another world, fruit meet for him. Liberality to the poor saints, to the poor world; a life in word and deed exemplary; a patient and quiet enduring of all things, till I have done and suffered the whole will of God, which he hath appointed for me. 'That on the good ground are they which, in an honest and good heart, having heard the word, keep it, and bring forth fruit with patience' (Luke 8:15). This is bringing forth fruit unto God; having our 'fruit unto holiness, and the end everlasting life' (Rom 7:4, 6:22, 14:8).

Fifth. The Lord expects fruit becoming the vineyard of God. 'The vineyard,' saith he, 'in a very fruitful hill': witness the fruit brought forth in all ages (Isa 5:1). The most barren trees that ever grew in the wood of this world, when planted in this vineyard by the God of heaven, what fruit to Godward have they brought forth! 'Abel offered the more excellent sacrifice' (Heb 11:4). Enoch walked with God three hundred years (Heb 11:5). Noah, by his life of faith, 'condemned the world, and became heir of the righteousness which is by faith' (Heb 11:7). Abraham left his country, and went out after God, not knowing whither he went (Heb 11:8). Moses left a kingdom, and run the hazard of the wrath of the king, for the love he had to God and Christ. What shall I say of them who had trials, 'not accepting deliverance, that they might obtain a better resurrection? They were stoned; they were sawn asunder; were tempted; were slain with the sword; they wandered about in sheep-skins and goat-skins, being destitute, afflicted, tormented' (Heb 11:35-37). Peter left his father, ship, and nets (Matt 4:18-20). Paul turned off from the feet of Gamaliel. Men brought their goods and possessions (the price of them) and cast it down at the apostle's feet (Acts 19:18-20). And others brought their books together, and burned them; curious books, though they were worth fifty thousand pieces of silver. I could add how many willingly offered themselves in all ages, and their all, for the worthy name of the Lord Jesus, to be racked, starved, hanged, burned, drowned, pulled in pieces, and a thousand calamities.[9] Barren fig-tree, the vineyard of God hath been a fruitful place. What dost thou there? What dost thou bear? God expects fruit according to, or becoming the soil of the vineyard.

Sixth. The fruit which God expecteth is such as becometh God's husbandry and labour. The vineyard is God's husbandry, or tillage. 'I am the true vine,' saith Christ, 'and my Father is the husbandman' (John 15:1). And again, 'Ye are God's husbandry, ye are God's building' (1 Cor 3:9). The vineyard; God fences it, God gathereth out the stones, God builds the tower, and the wine-press in the midst thereof. Here is labour, here is protection, here is removing of hindrances, here is convenient purgation, and all that there might be fruit.

Barren fig-tree, what fruit hast thou? Hast thou fruit becoming the care of God, the protection of God, the wisdom of God, the patience and husbandry of God? It is the fruit of the vineyard that is either the shame or the praise of the husbandman. 'I went by the field of the slothful,' saith Solomon, 'and by the vineyard of the man void of understanding; and lo, it was all grown over with thorns, and nettles had covered the face thereof' (Prov 34:30-32).

Barren fig-tree, if men should make a judgment of the care, and pains, and labour of God in his church, by the fruit that thou bringest forth, what might they say? Is he not slothful, is not he careless, is he not without discretion? O! thy thorns, thy nettles, thy barren heart and barren life, is a continual provocation to the eyes of his glory, as likewise a dishonour to the glory of his grace.

Barren fig-tree, hast thou heard all these things? I will add yet one more.

'And he came and sought fruit thereon.'

The question is not now, What thou thinkest of thyself, nor what all the people of God think of thee, but what thou shalt be found in that day when God shall search thy boughs for fruit? When Sodom was to be searched for righteous men, God would not, in that matter, trust his faithful servant Abraham; but still, as Abraham interceded, God answered, 'If I find fifty, - or forty and five there, I will not destroy the city' (Gen 18:20-28). Barren fig-tree, what sayest thou? God will come down to see, God will make search for fruit himself.

'And he came and sought fruit thereon, and found none. Then said he unto the dresser of the vineyard, Behold, these three years I come seeking fruit on this fig-tree, and find none; cut it down, why cumbereth it the ground?'

These words are the effects of God's search into the boughs of a barren fig-tree; he sought fruit, and found none—none to his liking, none pleasant and good. Therefore, first, he complains of the want thereof to the dresser; calls him to come, and see, and take notice of the tree; then signifieth his pleasure: he will have it removed, taken away, cut down from cumbering the ground.

Observe, The barren fig-tree is the object of God's displeasure; God cannot bear with a fruitless professor.

THEN said he, &c.

THEN, after this provocation; then, after he had sought and found no fruit, then. This word, THEN, doth show us a kind of an inward disquietness; as he saith also in another place, upon a like provocation. 'THEN the anger of the Lord, and his jealousy, shall smoke against that man, and all the curses that are written in this book shall lie upon him, and the Lord shall blot out his name from under heaven' (Deut 29:18-20).

THEN; it intimateth that he was now come to a point, to a resolution what to do with this fig-tree. 'Then said he to the dresser of this vineyard,' that is, to Jesus Christ, 'behold,' as much as to say, come hither, here is a fig-tree in my vineyard, here is a professor in my church, that is barren, that beareth no fruit.

Observe, However the barren professor thinks of himself on earth, the Lord cries out in heaven against him. 'And now go to, I will tell you what I will do to my vineyard: I will take away the hedge thereof, and it shall be eaten up; and I will break down the wall thereof, and it shall be trodden down' (Isa 5:5).

'Behold, THESE THREE YEARS I come seeking fruit.'

Observe, 'THESE THREE YEARS.' God cries out that this patience is abused, that his forbearance is abused. Behold, these three years I have waited, forborne; these three years I have deferred mine anger. 'Therefore will I stretch out my hand against thee, and destroy thee; I am weary with repenting' (Jer 15:6). 'These three years.' Observe, God layeth up all the time; I say, a remembrance of all the time that a barren fig-tree, or a fruitless professor, misspendeth in this world. As he saith also of Israel of old, 'forty years long was I grieved with this generation' (Psa 95:10).

'These three years,' &c. These three seasons: Observe, God remembers how many seasons thou hast misspent: for these three years signify so many seasons. And when the time of fruit drew nigh, that is, about the season they begin to be ripe, or that according to the season might so have been. Barren fig-tree, thou hast had time, seasons, sermons, ministers, afflictions, judgments, mercies, and what not; and yet hast not been fruitful. Thou hast had awakenings, reproofs, threatenings, comforts, and yet hast not been fruitful. Thou hast had patterns, examples, citations, provocations, and yet has not been fruitful. Well, God hath laid up thy three years with himself. He remembers every time, every season, every sermon, every minister, affliction, judgment, mercy, awakening, pattern, example, citation, provocation; he remembers all. As he said of Israel of old, 'They have tempted me now these ten times, and have not hearkened to my voice' (Num 14:22). And again, 'I remember all their wickedness' (Hosea 7:2).

'These three years,' &c. He seeks for the fruit of every season. He will not that any of his sermons, ministers, afflictions, judgments, or mercies, should be lost, or stand for insignificant things; he will have according to the benefit bestowed. (2 Chron 32:24,25). He hath not done without a cause all that he hath done, and therefore he looketh for fruit (Eze 14:23). Look to it, barren fig-tree.[10]

I came 'SEEKING' fruit.

Observe, This word 'SEEKING' signifies a narrow search; for when a man seeks for fruit on a tree, he goes round it and round it; now looking into this bough, and then into that; he peeks into the inmost boughs, and the lowermost boughs, if perhaps fruit may be thereon. Barren fig-tree, God will look into all thy boughs, he will be with thee in thy bed-fruits, thy midnight-fruits, thy closet-fruits, thy family-fruits, thy conversation-fruits, to see if there be any among all these that are fit for, or worthy of the name of the God of heaven. He sees 'what the ancients of the house of Israel do in the dark' (Eze 8:12). 'All things are naked and opened unto the eyes of him with whom we have to do' (Heb 4:12,13).

Seeking fruit on 'THIS' fig-tree.

I told you before, that he keeps in remembrance the times and seasons that the barren professor had wickedly misspent. Now, forasmuch as he also pointeth out the fig-tree, THIS fig-tree, it showeth that the barren professor, above all professors, is a continual odium in the eyes of God. This fig-tree, 'this man Coniah' (Jer 22:28). This people draw nigh me with their mouth, but have removed their hearts far from me. God knows who they are among all the thousands of Israel that are the barren and fruitless professors; his lot will fall upon the head of Achan, though he be hid among six hundred thousand men. 'And he brought his household, man by man, and Achan, the son of Carmi, the son of Zabdi, the son of Zera, of the tribe of Judah, was taken' (Josh 7:17,18). This is the Achan, this is the fig-tree, this is the barren professor!

There is a man hath a hundred trees in his vineyard, and at the time of the season, he walketh into his vineyard to see how the trees flourish; and as he goes, and views, and prys, and observes how they are hanged with fruit, behold, he cometh to one where he findeth naught but leaves. Now he makes a stand; looks upon it again and again; he looks also here and there, above and below; and if after all this seeking, he finds nothing but leaves thereon, then he begins to cast in his mind, how he may know this tree next year; what stands next it, or how far it is off the hedge? But if there be nothing there that may be as a mark to know it by, then he takes his hook, and giveth it a private mark—'And the Lord set a mark upon Cain' (Gen 4), saying, Go thy ways, fruitless fig-tree, thou hast spent this season in vain. Yet doth he not cut it down, I will try it another year: may be this was not a hitting[11] season. Therefore he comes again next year, to see if now it have fruit; but as he found it before, so he finds it now, barren, barren, every year barren; he looks again, but finds no fruit. Now he begins to have second thoughts, How! neither hit last year nor this? Surely the barrenness is not in the season; sure the fault is in the tree; however, I will spare it this year also, but will give it a second mark; and it may be he toucheth it with a hot iron, because he begins to be angry.

Well, at the third season he comes again for fruit, but the third year is like the first and second; no fruit yet; it only cumbereth the ground. What now must be done with this fig-tree? Why, the Lord will lop its boughs with terror; yea, the thickets of those professors with iron. I have waited, saith God, these three years; I have missed of fruit these three years; it hath been a cumber-ground these three years; cut it down. Precept hath been upon precept, and line upon line, one year after another, for these three years, but no fruit can be seen; I find none, fetch out the axe! I am sure THIS is the fig-tree, I know it from the first year; barrenness was its sign then, barrenness is its sign now; make it fit for the fire! Behold, 'now also the axe is laid unto the root of the trees: therefore, every tree that bringeth not forth good fruit, is hewn down, and cast into the fire' (Matt 3:10).

Observe, my brethren, God's heart cannot stand towards a barren fig-tree. You know thus it is with yourselves. If you have a tree in your orchard or vineyard that doth only cumber the ground, you cannot look upon that tree with pleasure, with complacency and delight. No; if you do but go by it, if you do but cast your eye upon it: yea, if you do but think of that tree, you threaten it in your heart, saying, I will hew thee down shortly; I will to the fire with thee shortly: and it is in vain for any to think of persuading of you to show favour to the barren fig-tree; and if they should persuade, your answer is irresistible, It yields me no profit, it takes up room and doth no good; a better may grow in its room.

Cut it down.

Thus, when the godly among the Jews made prayers that rebellious Israel might not be cast out of the vineyard, what saith the answer of God? (Jer 14:17). 'Though Moses and Samuel stood before me, yet my mind could not be toward this people': wherefore 'cast them out of my sight, and let them go forth' (Jer 15:1).

What a resolution is here! Moses and Samuel could do almost anything with God in prayer. How many times did Moses by prayer turn away God's judgments from even Pharaoh himself! yea, how many times did he by prayer preserve Israel, when in the wilderness, from the anger and wrath of God! (Psa 106:23). Samuel is reckoned excellent this way, yea, so excellent, that when Israel had done that fearful thing as to reject the Lord, and choose them another king, he prayed, and the Lord spared, and forgave them (1 Sam 12). But yet neither Moses nor Samuel can save a barren fig-tree. No; though Moses and Samuel stood before me, that is, pleading, arguing, interceding, supplicating, and beseeching, yet could they not incline mine heart to this people.

The Barren Fig Tree

Cut it down.

'Ay, but Lord, it is a fig-tree, a fig-tree!' If it was a thorn, or a bramble, or a thistle, the matter would not be much; but it is a fig-tree, or a vine. Well, but mark the answer of God, 'Son of man, What is the vine-tree more than any tree, or than a branch which is among the trees of the forest? Shall wood be taken thereof to do any work? or will men take a pin of it to hang any vessel thereon?' (Eze 15:2,3). If trees that are set, or planted for fruit, bring not forth that fruit, there is betwixt them and the trees of the forest no betterment at all, unless the betterment lieth in the trees of the wood, for they are fit to build withal; but a fig-tree, or a vine, if they bring not forth fruit, yea, good fruit, they are fit for nothing at all, but to be cut down and prepared for the fire; and so the prophet goes on, 'Behold, it is cast into the fire for fuel.' If it serve not for fruit it will serve for fuel, and so 'the fire devoureth both the ends of it, and the midst of it is burnt.'

Ay, but these fig-trees and vines are church-members, inhabiters of Jerusalem. So was the fig-tree mentioned in the text. But what answer hath God prepared for these objections? Why, 'Thus saith the Lord God, As the vine- tree among the trees of the forest, which I have given to the fire for fuel; so will I give the inhabitants of Jerusalem; and I will set my face against them, they shall go out from one fire, and another fire shall devour them' (Eze 15:6,7).

Cut it down.

The woman that delighteth in her garden, if she have a slip there, suppose, if it was fruitful, she would not take five pounds for it; yet if it bear no fruit, if it wither, and dwindle, and die, and turn cumber-ground only, it may not stand in her garden. Gardens and vineyards are places for fruit, for fruit according to the nature of the plant or flowers. Suppose such a slip as I told you of before should be in your garden, and there die, would you let it abide in your garden? No;

away with it, away with it! The woman comes into her garden towards the spring, where first she gives it a slight cast with her eye, then she sets to gathering out the weeds, and nettles, and stones; takes a besom and sweeps the walks; this done, she falls to prying into her herbs and slips, to see if they live, to see if they are likely to grow. Now, if she comes to one that is dead, that she is confident will not grow, up she pulls that, and makes to the heap of rubbish with it, where she despisingly casts it down, and valueth it no more than a nettle, or a weed, or than the dust she hath swept out of her walks. Yea, if any that see her should say, Why do you so? the answer is ready. It is dead, it is dead at root; if I had let it stand it would but have cumbered the ground. The strange slips, and also the dead ones, they must be 'a heap in the day of grief, and of desperate sorrow' (Isa 17:10,11).

Cut it down.

There are two manner of cuttings down; First. When a man is cast out of the vineyard. Second. When a man is cast out of the world.

First. When a man is cast out of the vineyard. And that is done two ways; 1. By an immediate hand of God. 2. By the church's due execution of the laws and censures which Christ for that purpose has left with his church.

1. God cuts down the barren fig-tree by an immediate hand, smiting his roots, blasting his branches, and so takes him away from among his people. 'Every branch,' saith Christ, 'that beareth not fruit in me, he,' my Father, 'taketh away' (John 15:2). He taketh him out of the church, he taketh him away from the godly. There are two things by which God taketh the barren professor from among the children of God: (1.) Strong delusions. (2.) Open profaneness.

(.1). By strong delusion; such as beguile the soul with damnable doctrines, that swerve from faith and godliness, 'They have chosen their own ways,' saith God, 'and their soul delighteth in their abominations. I also will choose their delusions, and will bring their fears upon them' (Isa 66:3,4). I will smite them with blindness, and hardness of heart, and failing of eyes; and will also suffer the tempter to tempt and affect his hellish designs upon them. 'God shall send them strong delusion, that they should believe a lie: that they all might be damned who believed not the truth, but had pleasure in unrighteousness' (2 Thess 2:10-12).

(2.) Sometimes God takes away a barren professor by open profaneness. There is one hath taken up a profession of that worthy name, the Lord Jesus Christ; but this profession is but a cloak; he secretly practiseth wickedness. He is a glutton, a drunkard, or covetous, or unclean. Well, saith God, I will loose the reins of this professor; I will give him up to his vile affections; I will loose the reins of his lusts before him; he shall be entangled with his beastly lusts; he shall be overcome of ungodly company. Thus they that turn aside to their own crooked ways 'the Lord shall lead them forth with the workers of iniquity' (Psa 125:5). This is God's hand immediately; God is now dealing with this man himself. Barren fig-tree, hearken! Thou art crowded into a profession, art got among the godly, and there art a scandal to the holy and glorious gospel; but withal so cunning that, like the sons of Zeruiah, thou art too hard for the church; she knows not how to deal with thee. Well, saith God, I will deal with that man myself, 'I will answer that man by myself.' He that sets up his idols in his heart, and puts the stumbling-block of his iniquity before his face, and yet comes and appears before me, 'I will set my face against that man, and will make him a sign and a proverb: and I will cut him off from the midst of my people; and ye shall know that I am the Lord' (Eze 14:7,8). But,

2. God doth sometimes cut down the barren fig-tree by the church, by the church's due execution of the laws and censures which Christ for that purpose hath left with his church. This is the meaning of that in Matthew 18; 1 Corinthians 5: and that in 1 Timothy 1:20

upon which now I shall not enlarge, But which way soever God dealeth with thee, O thou barren fig-tree, whither by himself immediately, or by his church, it amounts to one and the same; for if timely repentance prevent not, the end of that soul is damnation. They are blasted, and withered, and gathered by men, God's enemies; and at last being cast into the fire burning must be their end. 'That which beareth thorns and briars is nigh unto cursing, whose end is to be burned' (Heb 6:8).

Second. And, again, sometimes by 'Cut it down' God means, cast it out of the world. Thus he cut down Nadab and Abihu, when he burned them up with fire from heaven. Thus he cut down Korah, Dathan, and Abiram, when he made the earth to swallow them up (Num 3:4, 16:31-33). Thus he cut down Saul, when he gave him up to fall upon the edge of his own sword, and died (1 Sam 31:4). Thus he cut down Ananias, with Sapphira his wife, when he struck them down dead in the midst of the congregation (Acts 5:5,10). I might here also discourse of Absalom, Ahithophel, and Judas, who were all three hanged: the first by God's revenging hand, the others were given up of God to be their own executioners. These were barren and unprofitable fig-trees, such as God took no pleasure in, therefore he commanded to cut them down. The Psalmist saith, 'He shall take them away as with a whirlwind, both living, and in his wrath' (Psa 58:9). Barren fig-tree, hearken! God calls for the axe, his sword; bring it hither; here is a barren professor. Cut him down, why cumbereth he the ground?

Why cumbereth it the ground?

By these words the Lord suggesteth reasons of his displeasure against the barren fig-tree; it cumbereth the ground. The Holy Ghost doth not only take an argument from its barrenness, but because it is a cumber-ground, therefore cut it down; wherefore it must needs be a provocation. 1. Because, as much as in him lieth, he disappointeth the design of God in planting his vineyard; I looked that it should bring forth fruit. 2. It hath also abused his patience, his long-suffering, his three years' patience. 3. It hath also abused his labour, his pains, his care, and providence of protection and preservation: for he hedges his vineyard, and walls it about. Cumber-ground, all these things thou abusest! He waters his vineyard, and looks to it night and day; but all these things thou hast abused.

Further, there are other reasons of God's displeasure; as,

First. A cumber-ground is a very mock and reproach of religion, a mock and reproach to the ways of God, to the people of God, to the Word of God, and to the name of religion. It is expected of all hands, that all the trees in the garden of God should be fruitful: God expects fruit, the church expects fruit, the world, even the world, concludes that professors should be fruitful in good works; I say, the world expecteth that professors should be better than themselves. But, barren fig-tree, thou disappointest all. Nay, hast thou not learned the wicked ones thy ways? Hast thou not learned them to be more wicked by thy example?—but that is by the by. Barren fig-tree, thou hast disappointed others, and must be disappointed thyself! 'Cut it down, why cumbereth it the ground?'

Second. The barren fig-tree takes up the room where a better tree might stand; I say, it takes up the room, it keeps, so long as it stand where it doth; a fruitful tree out of that place, and therefore it must be cut down. Barren fig-tree, dost thou hear? Because the Jews stood fruitless in the vineyard, therefore, saith God, 'The kingdom of God shall be taken from you,' and given to a nation that shall render him their fruits in their season (Matt 21:33-41). The Jews for their barrenness were cut down, and more fruitful people put in their room. As Samuel also said to barren Saul, 'The Lord hath rent the kingdom from thee, and hath given it to a neighbour of thine that is better than thou' (1 Sam 15:28). The unprofitable servant must be cast out, must be cut down (Matt 25:27).

Cumber-ground, how many hopeful, inclinable, forward people, hast thou by thy fruitless and unprofitable life, kept out of the vineyard of God? For thy sake have the people stumbled at religion; by thy life have they been kept from the love of their own salvation. Thou hast been also a means of hardening others, and of quenching and killing weak beginnings. Well, barren fig-tree, look to thyself, thou wilt not go to heaven thyself, and them that would, thou hinderest; thou must not always cumber the ground, nor always hinder the salvation of others. Thou shalt be cut down, and another shall be planted in thy room.

Third. The cumber-ground is a sucker; he draws away the heart and nourishment from the other trees. Were the cumber ground cut down, the others would be more fruitful; he draws away that fatness of the ground to himself, that would make the others more hearty and fruitful. 'One sinner destroyeth much good' (Eccl 9:18).

The cumber-ground is a very drone in the hive, that eats up the honey that should feed the labouring bee; he is a thief in the candle, that wasteth the tallow, but giveth no light; he is the unsavoury salt, that is fit for nought but the dunghill. Look to it, barren fig-tree!

And he answering, said unto him, Lord, let it alone this year also, till I shall dig about it, and dung it; and if it bear fruit, well; and if not, then after that, thou shalt cut it down (vv 8,9).

These are the words of the dresser of the vineyard, who, I told you, is Jesus Christ, for he made intercession for the transgressors. And they contain a petition presented to an offended justice, praying, that a little more time and patience might be exercised towards the barren cumber- ground fig-tree.

In this petition there are six things considerable: 1. That justice might be deferred. O that justice might be deferred! 'Lord, let it alone,' &c., a while longer. 2. Here is time prefixed, as a space to try if more means will cure a barren fig-tree. 'Lord, let it alone this year also.' 3. The means to help it are propounded, 'until I shall dig about it, and dung it.'[12] 4. Here is also an insinuation of a supposition, that, by thus doing, God's expectation may be answered; 'and if it bear fruit, well.' 5. Here is a supposition that the barren fig-tree may yet abide barren, when Christ hath done what he will unto it; 'and if it bear fruit,' &c. 6. Here is at last a resolution, that if thou continue barren, hewing days will come upon thee; 'and if it bear fruit, well; and if not, then after that thou shalt cut it down.' But to proceed according to my former method, by way of exposition.

Lord, let it alone this year also.

Here is astonishing grace indeed! astonishing grace, I say, that the Lord Jesus should concern himself with a barren fig-tree; that he should step in to stop the blow from a barren fig-tree! True, he stopped the blow but for a time; but why did he stop it at all? Why did not he fetch out the axe? Why did he not do execution? Why did not he cut it down? Barren fig-tree, it is well for thee that there is a Jesus at God's right hand, a Jesus of that largeness of bowels, as to have compassion for a barren fig-tree, else justice had never let thee alone to cumber the ground as thou hast done! When Israel also had sinned against God, down they had gone, but that Moses stood in the breach. 'Let me alone,' said God to him, 'that I may consume them' in a moment, 'and I will make of thee a great nation' (Exo 32:10). Barren fig-tree, dost thou hear? Thou knowest not how oft the hand of Divine justice hath been up to strike, and how many years since thou hadst been cut down, had not Jesus caught hold of his Father's axe. Let me alone, let me fetch my blow, or 'Cut it down, why cumbereth it the ground?' Wilt thou not hear yet, barren fig-tree? Wilt thou provoke still? Thou hast wearied men, and provoked the justice of God! And 'will ye weary my God also?' (Isa 7:13).

Lord, let it alone this year.

Lord, a little longer! let us not lose a soul for want of means. I will try, I will see if I can make it fruitful, I will not beg a long life, nor that it might still be barren, and so provoke thee. I beg, for the sake of the soul, the immortal soul; Lord, spare it one year only, one year longer, this year also. If I do any good to it, it will be in little time. Thou shalt not be over wearied with waiting; one year and then.

Barren fig-tree, dost thou hear what a striving there is between the vine-dresser and the husbandman, for thy life? 'Cut it down,' says one; 'Lord, spare it,' saith the other. It is a cumber-ground, saith the Father; one year longer, prays the Son. 'Let it alone this year also.'

Till I shall dig about it, and dung it.

The Lord Jesus by these words supposeth two things, as causes of the want of fruit in a barren fig-tree; and two things he supposeth as a remedy.

The things that are a cause of want of fruit are, First. It is earth-bound. Lord, the fig-tree is earth-bound. Second. A want of warmer means, of fatter means. Wherefore, accordingly, he propoundeth to loosen the earth; to dig about it. And then to supply it with dung.

'To dig about it, and dung it. Lord, let it alone this year also, until I shall dig about it.' I doubt it is too much ground-bound. The love of this world, and the deceitfulness of riches lie too close to the roots of the heart of this professor (Luke 14). The love of riches, the love of honours, the love of pleasures, are the thorns that choke the word. 'For all that is in the world, the lust of the flesh, and the lust of the eyes, and the pride of life, is not of the Father,' but enmity to God; how then, where these things bind up the heart, can there be fruit brought forth to God? (1 John 2:15,16). Barren fig-tree, see how the Lord Jesus, by these very words, suggesteth the cause of thy fruitfulness of soul! The things of this world lie too close to thy heart; the earth with its things have bound up thy roots; thou art an

The Barren Fig Tree

earth-bound soul, thou art wrapped up in thick clay. 'If any man love the world, the love of the Father is not in him'; how then can he be fruitful in the vineyard? This kept Judas from the fruit of caring for the poor (John 12:6). This kept Demas from the fruit of self- denial (2 Tim 4:10). And this kept Ananias and Sapphira his wife from the goodly fruit of sincerity and truth (Acts 5:5,10). What shall I say? These are 'foolish and hurtful lusts, which drown men in destruction and perdition; for the love of money is the root of all evil.' How then can good fruit grow from such a root, the root of all evil? 'Which while some coveted after, they have erred from the faith, and pierced themselves through with many sorrows' (1 Tim 6:9,10). It is an evil root, nay, it is the root of all evil. How then can the professor that hath such a root, or a root wrapped up in such earthly things, as the lusts, and pleasures, and vanities of this world, bring forth fruit to God?

Till I shall 'DIG' about it.

Lord, I will loose his roots, I will dig up this earth, I will lay his roots bare; my hand shall be upon him by sickness, by disappointments, by cross providences; I will dig about him until he stands shaking and tottering; until he be ready to fall; then, if ever, he will seek to take faster hold. Thus, I say, deals the Lord Jesus ofttimes with the barren professor; he diggeth about him, he smiteth one blow at his heart, another blow at his lusts, a third at his pleasures, a fourth at his comforts, another at his self-conceitedness. Thus he diggeth about him; this is the way to take bad earth from his roots, and to loosen his roots from the earth. Barren fig- tree, see here the care, the love, the labour, and way, which the Lord Jesus, the dresser of the vineyard, is fain to take with thee, if haply thou mayest be made fruitful.[13]

Till I shall dig about it, and 'DUNG' it.

As the earth, by binding the roots too closely, may hinder the tree's being fruitful, so the want of better means may be also a cause thereof. And this is more than intimated by the dresser of the vineyard; 'Till I shall dig about it and dung it.' I will supply it with a more fruitful ministry, with a warmer word; I will give them pastors after mine own heart; I will dung them. You know dung is a more warm, more fat, more hearty, and succouring matter than is commonly the place in which trees are planted.

'I will dig about it, and dung it.' I will bring it under a heart-awakening ministry; the means of grace shall be fat and good: I will also visit it with heart-awakening, heart- warming, heart-encouraging considerations; I will apply warm dung to his roots; I will strive with him by my Spirit, and give him some tastes of the heavenly gift, and the power of the world to come. I am loth to lose him for want of digging. 'Lord, let it alone this year also, till I shall dig about it and dung it.'

And if it bear fruit, WELL.

And if the fruits of all my labour doth make this fig-tree fruitful, I shall count my time, my labour, and means, well bestowed upon it; and thou also, O my God, shalt be therewith much delighted; for thou art gracious, and merciful, and repentest thee of the evil which thou threatenest to bring upon a people. These words, therefore, inform us, that if a barren fig-tree, a barren professor, shall now at last bring forth fruit to God, it shall go well with that professor, it shall go well with that poor soul. His former barrenness, his former tempting of God, his abuse of God's patience and long-suffering, his mis-spending year after year, shall now be all forgiven him. Yea, God the Father, and our Lord Jesus Christ, will not pass by and forget all, and say, 'Well done,' at the last. When I say to the wicked, O wicked man, thou shalt surely die; if he then do that which is lawful and right, if he walk in the statutes of life, without committing iniquity, he shall surely live, he shall not die (Eze 33).

Barren fig-tree, dost thou hear? the axe is laid to thy roots, the Lord Jesus prays God to spare thee. Hath he been digging about thee? Hath he been dunging of thee? O barren fig-tree, now thou art come to the point; if thou shalt now become good, if thou shalt, after a gracious manner, suck in the gospel-dung, and if thou shalt bring forth fruit unto God, well; but if not, the fire is the last! fruit, or the fire; fruit, or the fire, barren fig-tree! 'If it bear fruit, well.'[14]

And if not, THEN after that thou shalt cut it down.

The Lord Jesus, by this if, giveth us to understand that there is a generation of professors in the world that are incurable, that will not, that cannot repent, nor be profited by the means of grace. A generation, I say, that will retain a profession, but will not bring forth fruit; a generation that will wear out the patience of God, time and tide, threatenings and intercessions, judgments and mercies, and after all will be unfruitful.

O the desperate wickedness that is in thy heart! Barren professor, dost thou hear? the Lord Jesus stands yet in doubt about thee; there is an IF stands yet in the way. I say, the Lord Jesus stands yet in doubt about thee, whether or no, at last, thou wilt be good; whether he may not labour in vain; whether his digging and dunging will come to more than lost labour; 'I gave her space to repent, - and she repented not' (Rev 2:21). I digged about it, I dunged it; I gained time, and supplied it with means; but I laboured herein in vain, and spent my strength for nought, and in vain! Dost thou hear, barren fig-tree? there is yet a question, Whether it may be well with thy soul at last?

And if not, THEN after that thou shalt cut it down.

There is nothing more exasperating to the mind of a man than to find all his kindness and favour slighted; neither is the Lord Jesus so provoked with anything, as when sinners abuse his means of grace; if it be barren and fruitless under my gospel; if it turn my grace into wantonness, if after digging and dunging, and waiting, it yet remain unfruitful, I will let thee cut it down.

Gospel means, applied, is the last remedy for a barren professor; if the gospel, if the grace of the gospel, will not do, there can be nothing expected but cut it down. 'Then after that thou shalt cut it down.' 'O Jerusalem, Jerusalem, thou that killest the prophets, and stonest them which are sent unto thee, how often would I have gathered thy children together, even as a hen gathereth her chickens under her wings, and ye would not!' Therefore 'your house is left unto you desolate' (Matt 23:37,38). Yet it cannot be, but that this Lord Jesus, who at first did put a stop to the execution of his Father's justice, because he desired to try more means with the fig-tree; I say, it cannot be, but that a heart so full of compassion as his is should be touched, to behold this professor must now be cut down. 'And when he was come near, he beheld the city, and wept over it, saying, If thou hadst known, even thou, at least in this thy day, the things which belong unto thy peace! but now they are hid from thine eyes' (Luke 19:41,42).

After that thou shalt cut it down.

When Christ giveth thee over, there is no intercessor, no mediator, no more sacrifice for sin, all is gone but judgment, but the axe, but a 'certain fearful looking for of judgment, and fiery indignation, which shall devour the adversaries' (Heb 10:26,27).

Barren fig-tree, take heed that thou comest not to these last words, for these words are a give up, a cast up, a cast up of a cast away; 'After that thou shalt cut it down.' They are as much as if Christ had said, Father, I begged for more time for this barren professor; I begged until I should dig about it, and dung it. But now, Father, the time is out, the year is ended, the summer is ended, and no good done! I have also tried with my means, with the gospel, I have digged about it; I have laid also the fat and hearty dung of the gospel to it, but all comes to nothing. Father, I deliver up this professor to thee again; I have done; I have done all; I have done praying and endeavouring; I will hold the head of thine axe no longer. Take him into the hands of justice; do justice; do the law; I will never beg for him more. 'After that thou shalt cut it down.' 'Woe also to them when I depart from them!' (Hosea 9:12). Now is this professor left naked indeed; naked to God, naked to Satan, naked to sin, naked to the law, naked to death, naked to hell, naked to judgment, and naked to the gripes of a guilty conscience, and to the torment of that worm that never dies, and to that fire that never shall be quenched. 'See that ye refuse not him that speaketh. For if they escaped not, who refused him that spake on earth, much more shall not we escape, if we turn away from him that speaketh from heaven' (Heb 12:25).

From this brief pass through this parable, you have these two general observations:—First. That even then when the justice of God cries out, I cannot endure to wait on this barren professor any longer, then Jesus Christ intercedes for a little more patience, and a little more striving with this professor, if possible he may make him a fruitful professor. 'Lord, let it alone this year also, till I shall dig about it, and dung it; and if it bear fruit, well,' &c. Second. There are some professors whose day of grace will end with, Cut it down, with judgment; when Christ, by his means, hath been used for their salvation.

First. The first of these observations I shall pass, and not meddle at all therewith; but shall briefly speak to the

Second, to wit, that there are some professors whose day of grace will end with, Cut it down, with judgment, when Christ, by his means, hath been used for their salvation.

This the apostle showeth in that third chapter of his Epistle to the Hebrews, where he tells us that the people of the Jews, after a forty years' patience and endeavour to do them good by the means appointed for that purpose, their end was to be cut down, or excluded the land of promise, for their final incredulity. 'So we see that they could not enter in, because of unbelief.' 'Wherefore,' saith he, 'I was grieved with that generation, and said, They do alway err in their heart, and they have not known my ways; so I sware in my wrath, They shall not enter into my rest.' As who should say, I would they should have entered in, and for that purpose I brought them out of Egypt, led them through the sea, and taught them in the wilderness, but they did not answer my work nor designs in that matter; wherefore they shall not, I swear they shall not. 'I sware in my wrath, they shall not enter into my rest.' Here is cutting down with judgment. So again, he saith, 'As I have sworn in my wrath, If they shall enter into my rest; although the works were finished from the foundation of the world' (Heb 4:4,5). This word 'if' is the same with 'they shall not,' in the chapter before. And where he saith, 'Although the works were finished from the foundation of the world,' he giveth us to understand that what preparations soever are made for the salvation of sinners, and of how long continuance soever they are, yet the God-tempting, God- provoking and fruitless professor, is like to go without a share therein, 'although the works were finished from the foundation of the world.' 'I will therefore put you in remembrance, though ye once knew this, how that the Lord having saved the people out of the land of Egypt, afterward destroyed them that believed not. And the angels that kept not their first estate, but left their own habitation, he hath reserved in everlasting chains under darkness, unto the judgment of the great day' (Jude 5,6). Here is an instance to purpose, an instance of men and angels: men saved out of the land of Egypt, and in their journey towards Canaan, the type of heaven, cut down; angels created and placed in the heavens in great estate and principality; yet both these, because unfruitful to God in their places, were cut down— the men destroyed by God, for so saith the text, and the 'angels reserved in everlasting chains under darkness, unto the judgment of the great day.'

Now, in my handling of this point, I shall discourse of the cutting down, or the judgment here denounced, as it respecteth the doing of it by God's hand immediately, and that too with respect to his casting them out of the world, and not as it respecteth an act of the church, &c. And as to this cutting down, or judgment, it must be concluded, that it cannot be before the day of grace be past with the fig-tree; but according to the observation, there are some professors whose day of grace will end with, Cut it down; and according to the words of the text, 'Then,' after that, 'thou shalt cut it down.' 'After that,' that is, after all my attempts and endeavours to make it fruitful, after I have left it, given it over, done with it, and have resolved to bestow no more days of grace, opportunities of grace, and means of grace upon it, then, 'after that,' thou shalt cut it down.

Besides, the giving up of the fig-tree is before the execution. Execution is not always presently upon the sentence given; for, after that, a convenient time is thought on, and then is cutting down. And so it is here in the text. The decree, that he shall perish, is gathered from its continuing fruitless quite through the last year—from its continuing fruitless at the end of all endeavours. But cutting down is not yet, for that comes with an afterward. 'Then, after that, thou shalt cut it down.'

So then, that I may orderly proceed with the observation, I must lay down these two propositions:—PROPOSITION FIRST. That the day of grace ends with some men before God takes them out of this world. And, PROPOSITION SECOND. The death, or cutting down of such men, will be dreadful. For this 'Cut it down,' when it is understood in the largest sense, as here indeed it ought, it showeth not only the wrath of God against a man's life in this world, but his wrath against him, body and soul; and is as much as to say, Cut him off from all the privileges and benefits that come by grace, both in this world and that which is to come. But to proceed:

PROPOSITION FIRST.—The day of grace ends with some men before God taketh them out of the world. I shall give you some instances of this, and so go on to the last proposition.

First. I shall instance Cain. Cain was a professor, a sacrificer, a worshipper of God, yea, the first worshipper that we read of after the fall; but his grapes were wild ones. His works were evil; he did not do what he did from true gospel motives, therefore God disallowed his work (Gen 4:3-8). At this his countenance falls, wherefore he envies his brother, disputes him, takes his opportunity, and kills him. Now, in that day that he did this act were the heavens closed up against him, and that himself did smartingly and fearfully feel when God made inquisition for the blood of Abel. 'And now art thou cursed,' said God, 'from the earth; which hath opened her mouth to receive thy brother's blood from thy hand,' &c. 'And Cain said, My punishment is greater than I can bear.' Mine iniquity is greater than that it may be forgiven. 'Behold thou hast driven me out this day from the face of the earth, and from thy face shall I be hid' (Gen 4:9-14). Now thou art cursed, saith God. Thou hast driven me out this day, saith Cain, and from thy face shall I be hid. I shall never more have hope in thee, smile from thee, nor expect mercy at thy hand. Thus, therefore, Cain's day of grace ended; and the heavens, with God's own heart, were shut up against him; yet after this he lived long. Cutting down was not come yet; after this he lived to marry a wife, to beget a cursed brood, to build a city, and what else I know not; all which could not be quickly done; wherefore Cain might live after the day of grace was past with him several hundred of years (Gen 4:10-17).

Second. I shall instance Ishmael. Ishmael was a professor, was brought up in Abraham's family, and was circumcised at thirteen years of age (Gen 16:12, 17:25,26). But he was the son of the bond-woman, he brought not forth good fruit; he was a wild professor. For all his religion, he would scoff at those that were better than himself. Well, upon a day his brother Isaac was weaned, at which time his father made a feast, and rejoiced before the Lord, for that he had given him the promised son; at this Ishmael mocked them, their son, and godly rejoicing. Then came the Spirit of God upon Sarah, and she cried, Cast him out, 'cast out this bond-woman and her son; for the son of this bond-woman shall not be heir with my son, with Isaac' (Gen 21:9-11). Now Paul to the Galatians makes this casting out to be, not only a casting out of Abraham's family, but a casting out also from a lot with the saints in heaven (Gal 4:29-31). Also Moses giveth us a notable proof thereof, in saying, that when he died he was gathered to his people—his people by his mother's side; for he was reckoned from her, the son of Hagar, the son of the bond-woman (Gen 25:17). Now, she came of the Egyptians, so that he was gathered when he died, notwithstanding his profession, to the place that Pharaoh and his host were gathered to, who were drowned in the Red Sea; these were his people, and he was of them, both by nature and disposition, by persecuting as they did (Gen 21:9).[15] But now, when did the day of grace end with this man? Observe, and I will show you. Ishmael was thirteen years old when he was circumcised, and then was Abraham ninety years old and nine (Gen 17:24-26). The next year Isaac was born; so that Ishmael was now fourteen years of age. Now, when Isaac was weaned, suppose he sucked four years, by that account, the day of grace must be ended with Ishmael by that time he was eighteen years old (Gen 25:12, &c.). For that day he mocked; that day it was said, 'Cast him out'; and of that casting out the apostle makes what I have said. Beware, ye young barren professors! Now, Ishmael lived a hundred and nineteen years after this, in great tranquility and honour with men. After this he also begat twelve princes, even after his day of grace was past.

Third. I shall instance Esau (Gen 25:27, &c.). Esau also was a professor; he was born unto Isaac, and circumcised according to the custom. But Esau was a gamesome professor, a huntsman, a man of the field; also he was wedded to his lusts, which he did also venture to keep, rather than the birthright. Well, upon a day, when he came from hunting, and was faint, he sold his birthright to Jacob, his brother. Now the birthright, in those days, had the promise and blessing annexed to it. Yea, they were so entailed in this, that the one could not go without the other; wherefore the apostle's caution is here of weight. Take heed, saith he, 'lest there be any fornicator, or profane person, as Esau, who for one morsel of meat sold his birthright. For ye know how that afterward, when he would have inherited the blessing, he was rejected; for he found no place of repentance, though he sought it carefully with tears' (Heb 12:16,17). Now, the ending of Esau's day of grace is to be reckoned from his selling of his birthright; for there the apostle points it, lest there be among you any that, like Esau, sells his birthright: for then goes hence the blessing also.

But Esau sold his birthright long before his death. Twenty years after this Jacob was with Laban, and when he returned home, his brother Esau met him (Gen 31:41, 32:4). Further, after this, when Jacob dwelt again some time with his father, then Jacob and Esau buried him. I suppose he might live above forty, yea, for ought I know, above fourscore years after he had sold his birthright, and so consequently had put himself out of the grace of God (Gen 35:28,29).[16]

Three things I would further note upon these three professors.

1. Cain, an angry professor; Ishmael, a mocking one; Esau, a lustful, gamesome one. Three symptoms of a barren professor; for he that can be angry, and that can mock, and that can indulge his lusts, cannot bring forth fruit to God.

2. The day of grace ended with these professors at that time when they committed some grievous sin. Cain's, when he killed his brother; Ishmael's, when he mocked at Isaac; and Esau's, when, out of love to his lusts, he despised and sold his birthright. Beware, barren professor! thou mayest do that in half a quarter of an hour, from the evil of which thou mayest not be delivered for ever and ever.[17]

3. Yet these three, after their day of grace was over, lived better lives, as to outward things, than ever they did before. Cain, after this, was lord of a city (Gen 4:17). Ishmael was, after this, father of twelve princes (Gen 25:16). And Esau, after this, told his brother, 'I have enough, my brother, keep that thou hast unto thyself' (Gen 33:8,9). Ease and peace, and a prosperous life in outwards, is no sign of the favour of God to a barren and fruitless professor, but rather of his wrath; that thereby he may be capable to treasure up more wrath against the day of wrath, and revelation of the righteous judgment of God. Let this much serve for the proof of the first proposition, namely, That the day of grace ends with some men before God takes them out of the world.

John Bunyan

SIGNS OF BEING PAST GRACE.

Now, then, to show you, by some signs, how you may know that the day of grace is ended, or near to ending, with the barren professor; and after that thou shalt cut it down. He that hath stood it out against God, and that hath withstood all those means for fruit that God hath used for the making of him, if it might have been, a fruitful tree in his garden, he is in this danger; and this indeed is the sum of the parable. The fig-tree here mentioned was blessed with the application of means, had time allowed it to receive the nourishment; but it outstood, withstood, overstood all, all that the husbandman did, all that the vine- dresser did.

But a little distinctly to particularize in four or five particulars.

First sign. The day of grace is like to be past, when a professor hath withstood, abused, and worn out God's patience, then he is in danger; this is a provocation; then God cries, 'Cut it down.' There are some men that steal into a profession nobody knows how, even as this fig-tree was brought into the vineyard by other hands than God's; and there they abide lifeless, graceless, careless, and without any good conscience to God at all. Perhaps they came in for the loaves, for a trade, for credit, for a blind; or it may be to stifle and choke the checks and grinding pangs of an awakened and disquieted conscience. Now, having obtained their purpose, like the sinners of Sion, they are at ease and secure; saying like Agag, 'Surely the bitterness of death is past' (1 Sam 15:22); I am well, shall be saved, and go to heaven. Thus in these vain conceits they spend a year, two, or three; not remembering that at every season of grace, and at every opportunity of the gospel the Lord comes seeking fruit. Well, sinner, well, barren fig-tree, this is but a coarse beginning: God comes for fruit.
1. What have I here? saith God; what a fig-tree is this, that hath

stood this year in my vineyard, and brought me forth no fruit? I will cry unto him, Professor, barren fig-tree, be fruitful! I look for fruit, I expect fruit, I must have fruit; therefore bethink thyself! At these the professor pauses; but these are words, not blows, therefore off goes this consideration from the heart. When God comes the next year, he finds him still as he was, a barren, fruitless cumber-ground. And now again he complains, here are two years gone, and no fruit appears; well, I will defer mine anger. 'For my name sake will I defer mine anger, and for my praise will I refrain for thee, that I cut thee not off,' as yet (Isa 48:9). I will wait, I will yet wait to be gracious. But this helps not, this hath not the least influence upon the barren fig-tree. Tush, saith he, here is no threatening: God is merciful, he will defer his anger, he waits to be gracious, I am not yet afraid (Isa 30:18). O! how ungodly men, that are at unawares crept into the vineyard, how do they turn the grace of our God into lasciviousness! Well, he comes the third year for fruit, as he did before, but still he finds but a barren fig-tree; no fruit. Now, he cries out again, O thou dresser of my vineyard, come hither; here is a fig-tree hath stood these three years in my vineyard, and hath at every season disappointed my expectation; for I have looked for fruit in vain; 'Cut it down,' my patience is worn out, I shall wait on this fig-tree no longer.

2. And now he begins to shake the fig-tree with his threatenings: Fetch out the axe! Now the axe is death; death therefore is called for. Death, come smite me this fig-tree. And withal the Lord shakes this sinner, and whirls him upon a sick-bed, saying, Take him, death, he hath abused my patience and forbearance, not remembering that it should have led him to repentance, and to the fruits thereof. Death, fetch away this fig-tree to the fire, fetch this barren professor to hell! At this death comes with grim looks into the chamber; yea, and hell follows with him to the bedside, and both stare this professor in the face, yea, begin to lay hands upon him; one smiting him with pains in his body, with headache, heart-ache, back-ache, shortness of breath, fainting, qualms, trembling of joints, stopping at the chest, and almost all the symptoms of a man past all recovery. Now, while death

is thus tormenting the body, hell is doing with the mind and conscience, striking them with its pains, casting sparks of fire in thither, wounding with sorrows, and fears of everlasting damnation, the spirit of this poor creature.[18] And now he begins to bethink himself, and to cry to God for mercy; Lord, spare me! Lord, spare me! Nay, saith God, you have been a provocation to me these three years.

How many times have you disappointed me? How many seasons have you spent in vain? How many sermons and other mercies did I, of my patience, afford you? but to no purpose at all. Take him, death! O! good Lord, saith the sinner, spare me but this once; raise me but this once. Indeed I have been a barren professor, and have stood to no purpose at all in thy vineyard; but spare! O spare this one time, I beseech thee, and I will be better! Away, away you will not; I have tried you these three years already; you are naught; if I should recover you again, you would be as bad as you were before. And all this talk is while death stands by. The sinner cries again, Good Lord, try me this once; let me get up again this once, and see if I do not mend. But will you promise me to mend? Yes, indeed, Lord, and vow it too; I will never be so bad again; I will be better. Well, saith God, death, let this professor alone for this time; I will try him a while longer; he hath promised, he hath vowed, that he will amend his ways. It may be he will mind to keep his promises. Vows are solemn things; it may be he may fear to break his vows. Arise from off they bed. And now God lays down his axe. At this the poor creature is very thankful, praises God, and fawns upon him, shows as if he did it heartily, and calls to others to thank him too. He therefore riseth, as one would think, to be a new creature indeed. But by that he hath put on his clothes, is come down from his bed, and ventured into the yard or shop, and there sees how all things are gone to sixes and sevens, he begins to have second thoughts, and says to his folks, What have you all been doing? How are all things out of order? I am I cannot tell what behind hand. One may see, if a man be but a little a to side, that you have neither wisdom nor prudence to order things.[19] And now, instead of seeking to spend the rest of his time to God, he doubleth his diligence after this world. Alas! all must not be lost; we must have provident care. And thus, quite forgetting the sorrows of death, the pains of hell, the promises and vows which he made to God to be better; because judgment was not now speedily executed, therefore the heart of this poor creature is fully set in him to do evil.

3. These things proving ineffectual, God takes hold of his axe again, sends death to a wife, to a child, to his cattle, 'Your young men have I slain, - and taken away your horses' (Amos 4:9,10). I will blast him, cross him, disappoint him, and cast him down, and will set myself against him in all that he putteth his hand unto. At this the poor barren professor cries out again, Lord, I have sinned; spare me once more, I beseech thee. O take not away the desire of mine eyes; spare my children, bless me in my labours, and I will mend and be better. No, saith God, you lied to me last time, I will trust you in this no longer; and withal he tumbleth the wife, the child, the estate into a grave. And then returns to his place, till this professor more unfeignedly acknowledgeth his offence (Hosea 5:14,15).

At this the poor creature is afflicted and distressed, rends his clothes, and begins to call the breaking of his promise and vows to mind; he mourns and prays, and like Ahab, awhile walks softly at the remembrance of the justness of the hand of God upon him. And now he renews his promises: Lord, try me this one time more; take off thy hand and see; they go far that never turn. Well, God spareth him again, sets down his axe again. 'Many times he did deliver them, but they provoked him with their counsel, and were brought low for their iniquity' (Psa 106:43). Now they seem to be thankful again, and are as if they were resolved to be godly indeed. Now they read, they pray, they go to meetings, and seem to be serious a pretty while, but at last they forget. Their lusts prick them, suitable temptations present themselves; wherefore they turn to their own crooked ways again. 'When he slew them, then they sought him, and they returned and inquired early after God'; 'nevertheless they did flatter him with their mouth, and they lied unto him with their tongue' (Psa 78:34-36).

4. Yet again, the Lord will not leave this professor, but will take up his axe again, and will put him under a more heart-searching ministry, a ministry that shall search him, and turn him over and over; a ministry that shall meet with him, as Elijah met with Ahab, in all his acts of wickedness, and now the axe is laid to the roots of the trees. Besides, this ministry doth not only search the heart, but presenteth the sinner with the golden rays of the glorious gospel; now is Christ Jesus s set forth evidently, now is grace displayed sweetly; now, now are the promises broken like boxes of ointment, to the perfuming of the whole room! But, alas! there is yet no fruit on this fig-tree. While his heart is searching, he wrangles; while the glorious grace of the gospel is unveiling, this professor wags and is wanton, gathers up some scraps thereof; 'Tastes the good Word of God, and the powers of the world to come'; 'drinketh in the rain that cometh oft upon him' (Heb 6:3-8; Jude 4). But bringeth not forth fruit meet for him whose gospel it is; 'Takes no heed to walk in the law of the Lord God of Israel with all his heart' (2 Kings 10:31). But counteth that the glory of the gospel consisteth in talk and show, and that our obedience thereto is a matter of speculation; that good works lie in good words; and if they can finely talk, they think they bravely please God. They think the kingdom of God consisteth only in word, not in power; and thus proveth ineffectual this fourth means also.

5. Well, now the axe begins to be heaved higher, for now indeed God is ready to smite the sinner; yet before he will strike the stroke, he will try one way more at the last, and if that misseth, down goes the fig-tree! Now this last way is to tug and strive with this professor by his Spirit. Wherefore the Spirit of the Lord is now come to him; but not always to strive with man (Gen 6:3). Yet a while he will strive with him, he will awaken, he will convince, he will call to

remembrance former sins, former judgments, the breach of former vows and promises, the misspending of former days; he will also present persuasive arguments, encouraging promises, dreadful judgments, the shortness of time to repent in; and that there is hope if he come. Further, he will show him the certainty of death, and of the judgment to come; yea, he will pull and strive with this sinner; but, behold, the mischief now lies here, here is tugging and striving on both sides. The Spirit convinces, the man turns a deaf ear to God; the Spirit saith, Receive my instruction and live, but the man pulls away his shoulder; the Spirit shows him whither he is going, but the man closeth his eyes against it; the Spirit offereth violence, the man strives and resists; they have 'done despite unto the Spirit of grace' (Heb 10:29). The Spirit parlieth a second time, and urgeth reasons of a new nature, but the sinner answereth, No, I have loved strangers, and after them I will go (Amos 4:6-12). At this God's fury comes up into his face: now he comes out of his holy place, and is terrible; now he sweareth in his wrath they shall never enter into his rest (Heb 3:11). I exercised towards you my patience, yet you have not turned unto me, saith the Lord. I smote you in your person, in your relations, in your estate, yet you have not returned unto me, saith the Lord. 'In thy filthiness is lewdness, because I have purged thee, and thou wast not purged; thou shalt not be purged from thy filthiness any more, till I cause my fury to rest upon thee' (Eze 24:13). 'Cut it down, why doth it cumber the ground?'

The second sign. That such a professor is almost, if not quite, past grace, is, when God hath given him over, or lets him alone, and suffers him to do anything, and that without control, helpeth him not either in works of holiness, or in straits and difficulties. 'Ephraim is joined to idols; let him alone' (Hosea 4:17). Woe be to them when I depart from them. I will laugh at their calamities, and will mock when their fear cometh (Prov 1:24-29).

Barren fig-tree, thou hast heretofore been digged about, and dunged; God's mattock hath heretofore been at thy roots; gospel-dung hath heretofore been applied to thee; thou hast heretofore been strove with, convinced, awakened, made to taste and see, and cry, O the blessedness! Thou hast heretofore been met with under the word; thy heart hath melted, thy spirit hath fallen, thy soul hath trembled, and thou hast felt something of the power of the gospel. But thou hast sinned, thou hast provoked the eyes of his glory, thy iniquity is found to be hateful, and now perhaps God hath left thee, given thee up, and lets thee alone. Heretofore thou wast tender; thy conscience startled at the temptation to wickedness, for thou wert taken off from 'the pollutions of the world, through the knowledge of the Lord and Saviour Jesus Christ' (2 Peter 2:20-22). But that very vomit that once thou wert turned from, now thou lappest up— with the dog in the proverb—again; and that very mire that once thou seemedst to be washed from, in that very mire thou now art tumbling afresh. But to particularize, there are three signs of a man's being given over of God.

1. When he is let alone in sinning, when the reins of his lusts are loosed, and he given up to them. 'And even as they did not like to retain God in their knowledge, God gave them over to a reprobate mind, to do those things which are not convenient: being filled with all unrighteousness' (Rom 1:28,29). Seest thou a man that heretofore had the knowledge of God, and that had some awe of Majesty upon him: I say, seest thou such an one sporting himself in his own deceivings, turning the grace of our God into lasciviousness, and walking after his own ungodly lusts? (Rom 1:30-31). His 'judgment now of a long time lingereth not, and his damnation slumbereth not' (2 Peter 2:13). Dost thou hear, barren professor? It is astonishing to see how those that once seemed 'sons of the morning,' and were making preparations for eternal life, now at last, for the rottenness of their hearts, by the just judgment of God, to be permitted, being past feeling, to give 'themselves over unto lasciviousness, to work all uncleanness with greediness' (Eph 4:18,19). A great number of such were in the first gospel-days; against whom Peter, and Jude, and John, pronounce the heavy judgment of God. Peter and Jude couple

them with the fallen angels, and John forbids that prayer be made for them, because that is happened unto them that hath happened to the fallen angels that fell, who, for forsaking their first state, and for leaving 'their own habitation,' are 'reserved in everlasting chains under darkness, unto the judgment of the great day' (Jude 5,6; 2 Peter 2:3-8). Barren fig-tree, dost thou hear? (1.) These are beyond all mercy! (2.) These are beyond all promises! (3.) These are beyond all hopes of repentance! (4.) These have no intercessor, nor any more share in a sacrifice for sin! (5.) For these there remains nothing but a fearful looking for of judgment! (6.) Wherefore these are the true fugitives and vagabonds, that being left of God, of Christ, of grace, and of the promise, and being beyond all hope, wander and straggle to and fro, even as the devil, their associate, until their time shall come to die, or until they descend in battle and perish!

2. Wherefore they are let alone in hearing. If these at any time come under the word, there is for them no God, no savour of the means of grace, no stirrings of heart, no pity for themselves, no love to their own salvation. Let them look on this hand or that, there they see such effects of the word in others as produceth signs of repentance, and love to God and his Christ. These men only have their backs bowed down alway (Rom 11:10). These men only have the spirit of slumber, eyes that they should not see, and ears that they should not hear, to this very day. Wherefore as they go to the place of the Holy, so they come from the place of the Holy, and soon are forgotten in the places where they so did (Eccl 8:10). Only they reap this damage, 'They treasure up wrath against the day of wrath, and revelation of the righteous judgment of God' (Rom 2:3-5). Look to it, barren professor!

3. If he be visited after the common way of mankind, either with sickness, distress, or any mind of calamity, still no God appeareth, no sanctifying hand of God, no special mercy is mixed with the affliction. But he falls sick, and grows well, like the beast; or is under distress, as Saul, who when he was engaged by the Philistines was

forsaken and left of God, 'And the Philistines gathered themselves together, and came and pitched in Shunem, and Saul gathered all Israel together, and they pitched in Gilboa. And when Saul saw the host of the Philistines he was afraid, and his heart greatly trembled. And when Saul inquired of the Lord, the Lord answered him not, neither by dreams, nor by Urim, nor by prophets' (1 Sam 28:4-6). The Lord answered him no more; he had done with him, cast him off, and rejected him, and left him to stand and fall with his sins, by himself. But of this more in the conclusion: therefore I here forbear.

4. These men may go whither they will, do what they will; they may range from opinion to opinion, from notion to notion, from sect to sect, but are steadfast nowhere; they are left to their own uncertainties, they have not grace to establish their hearts; and though some of them have boasted themselves of this liberty, yet Jude calls them 'wandering stars, to whom is reserved the blackness of darkness for ever' (Jude 13). They are left, as I told you before, to be fugitives and vagabonds in the earth, to wander everywhere, but to abide nowhere, until they shall descend to their own place, with Cain and Judas, men of the same fate with themselves (Acts 1:25).

A third sign that such a professor is quite past grace is, when his heart is grown so hard, so stony, and impenetrable, that nothing will pierce it. Barren fig-tree, dost thou consider? a hard and impenitent heart is the curse of God! A heart that cannot repent, is instead of all plagues at once; and hence it is that God said of Pharaoh, when he spake of delivering him up in the greatness of his anger, 'I will at this time,' saith he, 'send all my plagues upon thine heart' (Exo 9:14).

To some men that have grievously sinned under a profession of the gospel, God giveth this token of his displeasure; they are denied the power of repentance, their heart is bound, they cannot repent; it is impossible that they should ever repent, should they live a thousand years. It is impossible for those fall-aways to be renewed again unto repentance, 'seeing they crucify to themselves the Son of God afresh, and put him to an open shame' (Heb 6:4-6). Now, to have the heart so hardened, so judicially hardened, this is as a bar put in by the Lord God against the salvation of this sinner. This was the burden of Spira's complaint, 'I cannot do it! O! how I cannot do it!'[20]

This man sees what he hath done, what should help him, and what will become of him; yet he cannot repent; he pulled away his shoulder before, he stopped his ears before, he shut up his eyes before, and in that very posture God left him, and so he stands to this very day. I have had a fancy, that Lot's wife, when she was turned into a pillar of salt, stood yet looking over her shoulder, or else with her face towards Sodom; as the judgment caught her, so it bound her, and left her a monument of God's anger to after generations (Gen 19:26).

We read of some that are seared with a hot iron, and that are past feeling; for so seared persons in seared parts are. Their conscience is seared (1 Tim 4:2). The conscience is the thing that must be touched with feeling, fear, and remorse, if ever any good be done with the sinner. How then can any good be done to those whose conscience is worse than that? that is, fast asleep in sin (Eph 4:19). For that conscience that is fast asleep, may yet be effectually awakened and saved; but that conscience that is seared, dried, as it were, into a cinder, can never have sense, feeling, or the least regret in this world. Barren fig-tree, hearken, judicial hardening is dreadful! There is a difference betwixt that hardness of heart that is incident to all men, and that which comes upon some as a signal or special judgment of God. And although all kinds of hardness of heart, in some sense may be called a judgment, yet to be hardened with this second kind, is a judgment peculiar only to them that perish; hardness that is sent as a punishment for the abuse of light received, for a reward of apostasy. This judicial hardness is discovered from that which is incident to all men, in these particulars:—

1. It is a hardness that comes after some great light received, because

of some great sin committed against that light, and the grace that gave it. Such hardness as Pharaoh had, after the Lord had wrought wondrously before him; such hardness as the Gentiles had, a hardness which darkened the heart, a hardness which made their minds reprobate. This hardness is also the same with that the Hebrews are cautioned to beware of, a hardness that is caused by unbelief, and a departing from the living God; a hardness completed through the deceitfulness of sin (Heb 3:7, &c). Such as that in the provocation, of whom God sware, that they should not enter into his rest. It was this kind of hardness also, that both Cain, and Ishmael, and Esau, were hardened with, after they had committed their great transgressions.

2. It is the greatest kind of hardness; and hence they are said to be harder than a rock, or than an adamant, that is, harder than flint; so hard, that nothing can enter (Jer 5:3; Zech 7:12).

3. It is a hardness given in much anger, and that to bind the soul up in an impossibility of repentance.

4. It is a hardness, therefore, which is incurable, of which a man must die and be damned. Barren professor, hearken to this.

A fourth sign that such a professor is quite past grace, is, when he fortifies his hard heart against the tenor of God's word (Job 9:4, &c.) This is called hardening themselves against God, and turning of the Spirit against them. As thus, when after a profession of faith in the Lord Jesus, and of the doctrine that is according to godliness, they shall embolden themselves in courses of sin, by promising themselves that they shall have life and salvation notwithstanding. Barren professor, hearken to this! This man is called, 'a root that beareth gall and wormwood,' or a poisonful herb, such an one as is abominated of God, yea, the abhorred of his soul. For this man saith, 'I shall have peace, though I walk in the imagination' or stubbornness 'of mine heart, to add drunkenness to thirst'; an opinion flat against the whole Word of God, yea, against the very nature of God himself (Deut 29:18,19). Wherefore he adds, 'Then the anger of the Lord, and his jealousy, shall smoke against that man, and all the curses that are written in God's book shall lie upon him, and the Lord shall blot out his name from under heaven' (Deut 19:20).

Yea, that man shall not fail to be effectually destroyed, saith the text: 'The Lord shall separate that man unto evil, out of all the tribes of Israel, according to all the curses of the covenant' (Deut 19:21). He shall separate him unto evil; he shall give him up, he shall leave him to his heart; he shall separate him to that or those that will assuredly be too hard for him.

Now this judgment is much effected when God hath given a man up unto Satan, and hath given Satan leave, without fail, to complete his destruction. I say, when God hath given Satan leave effectually to complete his destruction; for all that are delivered up unto Satan have not, nor do not come to this end. But that is the man whom God shall separate to evil, and shall leave in the hands of Satan, to complete, without fail, his destruction.

Thus he served Ahab, a man that sold himself to work wickedness in the sight of the Lord. 'And the Lord said, Who shall persuade Ahab, that he may go up and fall at Ramoth-Gilead? And one said on this manner, and another said on that manner. And there came forth a spirit, and stood before the Lord, and said, I will persuade him. And the Lord said unto him, Wherewith? And he said, I will go forth, and be a lying spirit in the mouth of all his prophets. And he said, Thou shalt persuade him, and prevail also; go forth, and do so' (1 Kings 21:25, 22:20-22). Thou shalt persuade him, and prevail; do thy will, I leave him in thy hand, go forth, and do so.

Wherefore, in these judgments the Lord doth much concern himself for the management thereof, because of the provocation wherewith they have provoked him. This is the man whose ruin contriveth, and bringeth to pass by his own contrivance: 'I also will choose their delusions' for them; 'I will bring their fears upon them' (Isa 66:4). I will choose their devices, or the wickednesses that their hearts are contriving of. I, even I, will cause them to be accepted of, and delightful to them. But who are they that must thus be feared? Why, those among professors that have chosen their own ways, those whose soul delighteth in their abominations. Because they received not the love of the truth, that they might be saved: for this cause God shall send them strong delusions, that they should believe a lie, that they all might be damned, who believed not the truth, but had pleasure in unrighteousness.

'God shall send them.' It is a great word! Yea, God shall send them strong delusions; delusions that shall do: that shall make them believe a lie. Why so? 'That they all might be damned,' every one of them, 'who believed not the truth, but had pleasure in unrighteousness' (2 Thess 2:10- 12).

There is nothing more provoking to the Lord, than for a man to promise when God threateneth; for a man to delight of conceit that he shall be safe, and yet to be more wicked than in former days, this man's soul abhorreth the truth of God; no marvel, therefore, if God's soul abhorreth him; he hath invented a way contrary to God, to bring about his own salvation; no marvel, therefore, if God invent a way to bring about this man's damnation: and seeing that these rebels are at this point, we shall have peace; God will see whose word will stand, his or theirs.

A fifth sign of a man being past grace is, when he shall at this scoff, and inwardly grin and fret against the Lord, secretly purposing to continue his course, and put all to the venture, despising the messengers of the Lord. 'He that despised Moses' law, died without mercy; - of how much sorer punishment, suppose ye, shall he be thought worthy, who hath trodden under foot the Son of God?' &c. (Heb 10:28). Wherefore, against these despisers God hath set himself, and foretold that they shall not believe, but perish: 'Behold, ye despisers, and wonder, and perish: for I work a work in your days, a work which ye shall in nowise believe, though a man declare it unto you' (Acts 13:41).

After that thou shalt cut it down.

Thus far we have treated of the barren fig-tree, or fruitless professor, with some signs to know him by; whereto is added also some signs of one who neither will nor can, by any means, be fruitful, but they must miserably perish. Now, being come to the time of execution, I shall speak a word to that also; 'After that thou shalt cut it down.'

PROPOSITION SECOND. The death or cutting down of such men will be dreadful.

Christ, at last, turns the barren fig-tree over to the justice of God, shakes his hands of him, and gives him up to the fire for his unprofitableness. 'After that thou shalt cut it down.'

Two things are here to be considered:

First. The executioner; thou, the great, the dreadful, the eternal God. These words, therefore, as I have already said, signify that Christ the Mediator, through whom alone salvation comes, and by whom alone execution hath been deferred, now giveth up the soul, forbears to speak one syllable more for him, or to do the least act of grace further, to try for his recovery; but delivereth him up to that fearful dispensation, 'to fall into the hands of the living God' (Heb 10:31).

Second. The second to be considered is, The instrument by which this execution is done, and that is death, compared here to an axe; and forasmuch as the tree is not felled at one blow, therefore the strokes are here continued, till all the blows be struck at it that are requisite for its felling: for now cutting time, and cutting work, is come; cutting must be his portion till he be cut down. 'After that thou shalt cut it down.' Death, I say, is the axe, which God often useth, therewith to take the barren fig-tree out of the vineyard, out of a profession, and also out of the world at once. But this axe is now new ground, it cometh well-edged to the roots of this barren fig-tree. It hath been whetted by sin, by the law, and by a formal profession, and therefore must, and will make deep gashes, not only in the natural life, but in the heart and conscience also of this professor: 'The wages of sin is death,' 'the sting of death is sin' (Rom 6:23; 1 Cor 15:56). Wherefore death comes not to this man as he doth to saints, muzzled, or without his sting, but with open mouth, in all his strength; yea, he sends his first-born, which is guilt, to devour his strength, and to bring him to the king of terrors (Job 18:13,14).

But to give you, in a few particulars, the manner of this man's dying.

1. Now he hath his fruitless fruits beleaguer him round his bed, together with all the bands and legions of his other wickedness. 'His own iniquities shall take the wicked himself, and he shall be holden with the cords of his sins' (Prov 5:22).

2. Now some terrible discovery of God is made out unto him, to the perplexing and terrifying of his guilty conscience. 'God shall cast upon him, and not spare'; and he shall be 'afraid of that which is high' (Job 27:22; Eccl 12:5).

3. The dark entry he is to go through will be a sore amazement to him; for 'fears shall be in the way' (Eccl 12:5). Yea, terrors will take hold on him, when he shall see the yawning jaws of death to gape upon him, and the doors of the shadow of death open to give him passage out of the world. Now, who will meet me in this dark entry? how shall I pass through this dark entry into another world?

4. For by reason of guilt, and a shaking conscience, his life will hang

in continual doubt before him, and he shall be afraid day and night, and shall have no assurance of his life (Deut 28:66,67).

5. Now also want will come up against him; he will come up like an armed man. This is a terrible army to him that is graceless in heart, and fruitless in life. This WANT will continually cry in thine ears, Here is a new birth wanting, a new heart, and a new spirit wanting; here is faith wanting; here is love and repentance wanting; here is the fear of God wanting, and a good conversation wanting: 'Thou art weighed in the balances, and art found wanting' (Dan 5:27).

6. Together with these standeth by the companions of death, death and hell, death and evils, death and endless torment in the everlasting flames of devouring fire. 'When God cometh up unto the people he will invade them with his troops' (Hab 3:16).

But how will this man die? Can his heart now endure, or can his hands be strong? (Eze 22:14).

(1.) God, and Christ, and pity, have left him. Sin against light, against mercy, and the long-suffering of God, is come up against him; his hope and confidence now lie a-dying by him, and his conscience totters and shakes continually within him!

(2.) Death is at his work, cutting of him down, hewing both bark and heart, both body and soul asunder. The man groans, but death hears him not; he looks ghastly, carefully, dejectedly; he sighs, he sweats, he trembles, but death matters nothing.

(3.) Fearful cogitations haunt him, misgivings, direful apprehensions of God, terrify him. Now he hath time to think what the loss of heaven will be, and what the torments of hell will be: now he looks no way but he is frighted.

(4.) Now would he live, but may not; he would live, though it were but the life of a bed-rid man, but he must not. He that cuts him down sways him as the feller of wood sways the tottering tree; now this way, then that, at last a root breaks, a heart-string, an eye-string, sweeps asunder.

(5.) And now, could the soul be annihilated, or brought to nothing, how happy would it count itself, but it sees that may not be. Wherefore it is put to a wonderful strait; stay in the body it may not, go out of the body it dares not. Life is going, the blood settles in the flesh, and the lungs being no more able to draw breath through the nostrils, at last out goes the weary trembling soul, which is immediately seized by devils, who lay lurking in every hole in the chamber for that very purpose. His friends take care of the body, wrap it up in the sheet or coffin, but the soul is out of their thought and reach, going down to the chambers of death.

I had thought to have enlarged, but I forbear. God, who teaches man to profit, bless this brief and plain discourse to thy soul, who yet standest a professor in the land of the living, among the trees of his garden. Amen.

FOOTNOTES:

[1] General Doctrine of Toleration, 8vo, 1781.

[2] This awful destruction of Jerusalem by the Romans is narrated by Josephus in his sixth book of the Jewish Wars, in language that makes nature shudder. Multitudes had assembled to celebrate the passover when the invading army beleaguered the city; a frightful famine soon filled it with desolation: this, with fire and sword, miserably destroyed one million, three hundred and thirty-seven thousand, four hundred and ninety Jews, while the Christians fled before the siege, and escaped to the mountains. Well might the sun vail his face at that atrocious deed, which was so quickly followed by such awful punishment.—Ed.

[3] Reader, do not imagine that this was peculiar to Bunyan's days;

look not upon your neighbours to find an example, but search your own heart—'Lord, is it I?' and strive and pray that you may bring forth more fruit.—Ed.

[4] The mode of admitting a member to church-fellowship, among the Baptists, was and now is by introducing the trembling convert to a private meeting of the whole church, that they may hear why the union is sought, how the soul became alarmed, and fled for refuge to Christ, with the grounds of hope; inquiries having been previously made into Christian character and godliness. If, with all these precautions, a barren professor gains admittance, the punishment is not upon the garden, but upon the barren tree.—Ed.

[5] 'Humour,' the temper or disposition of mind. Not out of love to humility, but these creeping things pretend to be humble, to gain some sinister end.—Ed.

[6] However strange it may appear, it is true that the Ranters, in Bunyan's time, used these arguments, and those so graphically put into the mouth of Bye-ends, in the Pilgrim, to justify their nonconformity to Christ. The tom- fooleries and extravagancies of dress introduced by Charles II, are here justly and contemptuously described. The ladies' head-dresses, called 'frizzled fore-tops,' became so extravagant, that a barber used high steps to enable him to dress a lady's head!—Ed.

[7] A word not to be found in our dictionaries, being local and almost obsolete. It means a division, end, or border of a town or village.—Ed.

[8] See the character of Talkative, in the Pilgrim's Progress. 'His house is as empty of religion as the white of an egg is of savour. There is in his house neither prayer, nor sign of repentance for sin. He is the very stain, reproach, and shame of religion. Thus say the common people that know him, A saint abroad and a devil at home.'—Ed.

The Barren Fig Tree

[9] How great is the mercy that those horrid barbarities, perpetrated upon peaceful Christians, are now only heard of in those distance parts of Satan's empire, China and Madagascar! Has the enmity of the human heart by nature changed? No; but the number of Christians has so vastly increased with a civilizing influence, as to change the face of society. What a paradise will this earth become when Christ shall reign in every heart!—Ed.

[10] In the midst of these faithful admonitions, we venture to remark that, according to Lightfoot, so valuable was the fig-tree that it was never destroyed until means were carefully used to restore its fruitfulness, and that the use of these means occupied a period of three years. This illustrates the wisdom of our Lord in selecting the fig-tree as the principal object presented to view in his parable. It is a most valuable tree—capable of bearing much fruit; still, after every trial, if it remains barren, it must be cut down as a cumber-ground, and sent to the fire.—Ed.

[11] A 'hit,' in some parts of the country, is used to express a good crop. A 'hitting season' means a fruitful season.— Ed.

[12] This mode of infusing new vigour into plants and trees is thus described in the Gemara—'They lay dung in their gardens, to soften the earth. They dig about the roots of their trees, and sprinkle ashes, and pluck up suckers, and make a smoke beneath to kill vermin.'—Ed.

[13] Among the superstitions of the ancients, Michaelis states that both the Greeks and Asiatics had a superstition that a tree might be rendered fruitful by striking it, at the intercession of a friend, three times with the back of an axe.—Ed.

[14] However painfully unpleasant these terms may appear to eyes or ears polite, it is a homely but just representation, and calculated to make a lasting impression on every reader. Afflictions, trials, crosses,

are used as a means of creating or reviving spiritual life, as manure is applied to vegetation.—Ed.

[15] Mahomet professed descent from Ishmael, and that he came to revive the religion which God had revealed to Abraham, who taught it to Ishmael. Mahometanism is the religion of the outcast of God.—Ed.

[16] Bunyan had been haunted with the temptation 'to sell and part with Christ,' and, under a fear that he had fallen under that temptation, the case of Esau made a dreadful impression upon his soul; extreme horror and anguish seized upon his spirit; 'he was like a man bereft of life and bound over to eternal punishment,' for two years. At length, after an awful storm, he found peace in the promise, 'his blood cleanseth from ALL sins,' and a proof that he had not sold Christ.—See Grace Abounding, No. 139-160.

[17] How solemn a thought! What an appeal to perpetual watchfulness. Why have I not made shipwreck of faith? Most emphatically may we reply, Because God has sustained my soul.—Ed.

[18] Bunyan's tongue and pen are here fired by his vivid imagination of eternal realities. With such burning words, we need no messenger from the invisible world to alarm the consciences of sinners. What angel could arouse more powerfully, alarmingly, convincingly, the poor sinner, than the whole of this chain of reasoning.—Ed.

[19] This picture is drawn by a master hand: the master is laid by for a season; or, as Bunyan quaintly expresses it, 'a little a to side': when raised from affliction earthly affairs absorb his attention, and he forgets his good resolves. According to the old rhyme:—

'The devil was sick, the devil a saint would be
The devil to well, the devil a saint was he.'—Ed.

[20] This is referred to in the Pilgrim, at the Interpreter's house, by

the representation of a man in an iron cage, who says, 'I cannot get out, O now I cannot!' The awful account of Spira's despair must have made a strong impression upon Bunyan's mind. It commences with a poem.

'Here see a soul that's all despair;
a man All hell; a spirit all wounds; who can
A wounded spirit bear?
Reader, would'st see, what may you never feel
Despair, racks, torments, whips of burning steel!
Behold, the man's the furnace, in whose heart
Sin hath created hell; O in each part
What flames appear:
His thoughts all stings; words, swords;
Brimstone his breath;
His eyes flames; wishes curses, life a death;
A thousand deaths live in him, he not dead;
A breathing corpse in living, scalding lead.' —Fearful Estate of Francis Spira.—Ed.

John Bunyan

The Barren Fig Tree

John Bunyan